AMERICAN NATURE GUIDES

SEASHELLS

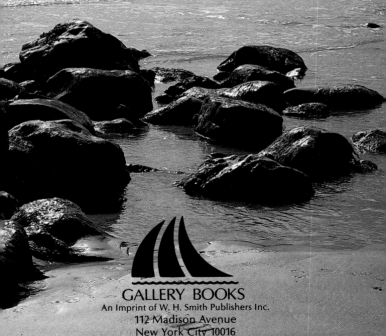

AMERICAN NATURE GUIDES

SEASHELLS

R. TUCKER ABBOTT

GALLERY BOOKS
An Imprint of W. H. Smith Publishers Inc.
112 Madison Avenue
New York City 10016

This edition first published in 1990 by Gallery Books,
an imprint of W. H. Smith Publishers, Inc.,
112 Madison Avenue, New York 10016

Published in England by Dragon's World Ltd,
Limpsfield and London

Editor: Diana Steedman
Designer: David Hunter
Editorial Director: Pippa Rubinstein

Gallery Books are available for bulk purchase for sales
promotions and premium use. For details write or telephone
the Manager of Special Sales, W. H. Smith Publishers, Inc.,
112 Madison Avenue, New York, New York 10016.
(212) 532-6600.

ISBN 0 8317 6967 X

Printed in Singapore

Contents

Introduction

For our great grandparents conchology, the study of shells and shellfish, was a pleasant and inspirational pastime that taught them about newly discovered shells from exotic seas. The bounties of nature were for the taking. But, with man's burgeoning populations, and the pollution of our shorelines, the modern study of shellfish, malacology, has developed to help combat the effects of oil spills, toxic drainage and other radical disturbances to the ecology of the world's molluscs.

The Phylum Mollusca
The phylum Mollusca includes seashells, squid and octopuses, as well as terrestrial and freshwater snails and clams, and outnumbers all the vertebrate species. The estimated 80,000 species of molluscs are a main source of food for fish, birds and man. Along our sandy or rocky shores they dominate marine life. Their populations are a barometer of the health of our seas.

The Arctic Ocean and the warmer seas that border it are a natural path for the interchange of circumpolar species. But the further south one goes, the more separate and distinct become the faunas in the warmer waters that are isolated by continental masses. While the life cycle of many snails and clams includes free-swimming stages that permit far-flung distributions, there are many molluscs that lay stationary egg capsules or give birth to live, crawling young. These different patterns of shell populations eventually lead to subspecies unique to small, isolated places.

This pocket guide offers a selection of the most frequently encountered types of molluscs found in the northern Pacific and Atlantic. Three major regions are covered: the north eastern Pacific from the Aleutian Islands and Alaska, south to Oregon; the north western Atlantic from Labrador to approximately Virginia; and the north eastern Atlantic from Scandinavia to Portugal.

How and Where Shells Live
Water temperature, substrate and wave action are the three primary factors influencing the nature of molluscan populations. Shorelines in Arctic and boreal regions are largely destitute of shells because of the grinding effect of seasonal ice cover. Offshore and under the ice there is a fairly rich fauna. In

more temperate waters, protected back bays and tidepools along rocky coasts teem with marine life, although the number of species is relatively low.

Understanding the various species' habitat preferences makes locating them much easier. Some periwinkles and dogwinkles are hidden under festoons of rock-clinging algae; other snails are found only among clusters of barnacles and mussels; and the mud-loving nassa snails abound on intertidal flats. An old floating log, when broken apart, may reveal several species of wood-boring bivalves, and clinging to the underside of some sea stars and sea-urchins may be found tiny parasitic snails and clams. In identifying species it should be realized that in some cases certain species change shape as they grow older. Some univalves develop a thickened or expanded outer lip when they reach maturity. Diet and water conditions, as well as boring sponges and marauding crabs and fish, can alter the condition of the shell.

The Eastern Pacific, or western coast of North America, is bounded by the Arctic Sea where about 110 species can be obtained only by dredging from a boat or investigating wearing winter scuba gear. Southward, in the Aleutian subprovince, collecting improves and many species common to northern Japan and southern Alaska are readily obtained in shallow water. Below this is the Oregonian Province, one of the richest areas in the world for numbers of molluscan specimens. The temperate waters from northern British Columbia to Oregon and the northern sections of California are rich in rock-dwelling limpets, dogwinkles and mussels.

On the eastern coast of North America, the inhospitable shores of Hudson Bay, Labrador, Greenland and northern Iceland are relatively barren, although offshore waters support a respectable community of polar species. The Acadian subprovince, extending from Newfoundland and the Maritime Provinces south to Cape Cod, is fairly rich in shallow-water and shore species. There is a vast variation in habitats, from the extensive, intertidal mud flats of the Bay of Fundy to the gravel bottoms of Georges Banks and the sandy beaches of Cape Cod.

Western Europe, or the Eastern Atlantic, is also a mixture of major faunal elements. The conditions in northern Scandinavia and the Shetland Islands are as severe as those in northern Alaska. The Celtic Province, encompassing the British Isles, the Baltic Sea and France, is much richer and, indeed, has some elements that have invaded from the warmer Mediterranean Province, especially around northern Portugal. Occasionally, warmer-water, pelagic species are wafted on to the southern shores of England.

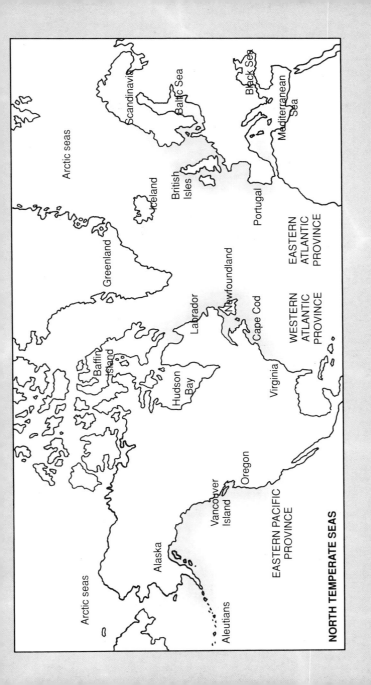

NORTH TEMPERATE SEAS

Arctic seas

Scandinavia

Baltic Sea

Black Sea

Mediterranean Sea

Arctic seas

Iceland

British Isles

Portugal

Greenland

EASTERN ATLANTIC PROVINCE

Newfoundland

Labrador

Cape Cod

WESTERN ATLANTIC PROVINCE

Baffin Island

Hudson Bay

Virginia

Oregon

Vancouver Island

EASTERN PACIFIC PROVINCE

Alaska

Aleutians

Arctic seas

Common to most of these provinces in the northern hemisphere are many species of pelagic squids and tiny pteropod gastropods, all of which serve as an important source of food for fish and whales. Many shell-less sea-slugs, or nudibranchs, are common to England and New England. On the deep slopes of the continents, at many hundreds of feet in depth, there are many species of molluscs that have a circumpolar distribution because of the similar dark, cold conditions around the globe at those high latitudes.

Collecting Shells

While modest collecting of live specimens has less effect than nature's normal pruning by predation, aging and natural ecological changes, today there are more and more naturalists who prefer to hunt with camera or observe molluscs at close range in aquariums. But well-executed surveys and censuses must be backed by a sampling of correctly identified specimens. Provided you take only what you need, building a personal, well-documented shell collection is a pleasure and a useful project.

Shells with soft parts may be cleaned by boiling them in water for five minutes or placing them in a plastic, open bag in the microwave oven set on high for two minutes. The best preservative for very small shells or large soft parts is 70% grain alcohol. Formalin, unless well-buffered, will etch and eventually dissolve calcium carbonate shells. Geographical and ecological data should be recorded in a catalogue and be repeated on good label paper to accompany the india ink-numbered shells. Arrange the collection in phylogenetic order, the sequence in which most shell guides, including this one, are organized.

How to Use this Book

This pocket guide provides photographic color reference along with descriptive details covering special features, measurement, and distribution for over 370 shells which can be found along the west coast and the eastern seaboard of the USA, and the northern and western coasts of Europe. The various families of molluscs are arranged in a standard biological order, with the more primitive, or simpler, species presented first, followed by the more advanced kinds. But this is still only a small proportion of the vast array of molluscs that exist. To serve as a bridge to the more complete works, a bibliography appears on page 172, while the glossary on pages 11-14 defines the words used in the descriptions.

Glossary

While many unfamiliar nouns and adjectives used in conchology may be found in dictionaries, for the convenience of collectors and observers in the field, a brief glossary of the most frequently used words in our shell descriptions is included here. Those words *italicised* are also defined.

Adductor muscle (in *bivalves*). Large muscle inside the shell that closes the two valves.
Anterior end Front end; in *univalves*, the head or *siphonal end*; in *bivalves*, where the foot usually protrudes.
Aperture The opening in the last *whorl*, providing an outlet for the head and foot of a snail.
Apex The first-formed, narrow end of a snail shell, usually of several *whorls*.
Axial Parallel to the lengthwise axis of a shell; *suture* to suture features.

Base The lower *siphonal end* of the body or last *whorl*; opposite the *apex*.
Beak (or *umbo*) The first formed part of a *bivalve's* valve, usually above the *hinge*.
Bivalve A member of the class Bivalvia (or Pelecypoda), such as a clam or oyster.
Body whorl The largest and most recently formed *whorl*.
Boreal Relating to the northern climatic zone.
Byssus A clump of horny threads spun by the foot of a *bivalve* and used for attachment.

Callus A thickening, usually of shelly material.
Cancellate Marked by crossing lines, like latticework.
Chitinous Horny or corneous, usually soft and flexible material making up an *operculum*.
Chondrophore Spoon-shaped shelf in the *hinge* of a *bivalve*.
Circumpolar Found around either the North or South Pole.
Columella The solid pillar at the *axis* of the *univalve* shell, around which the *whorls* grow.
Concentric Sculpturing of ridges, ribs or threads, or color markings, running parallel to the margins of a *bivalve* or *operculum*.

Dextral Right-handed or of *whorls* growing clockwise. *Aperture* at right if *apex* is held uppermost.

Escutcheon   A smooth, long surface on the upper margin of the *valve* of a *bivalve* behind the *ligament*.

Fimbriated   Having thin, wavy, rough, fringed borders.
Fusiform   Shaped like a spindle, swollen in the center, narrow as each end.

Gape   Opening between the margins of the *valves* when the *bivalve* is shut.
Gastropod   A mollusc possessing a single shell (*univalve*).
Globular   Bulbous, or shaped like a round globe.

Head scar   Muscular attachment scar inside a limpet.
Hinge   Top margin of a *bivalve* where shelly teeth interlock.

Inner lip   The wall on the body *whorl* opposite the outer lip of the *aperture*.
Intertidal   Area between high and low tide mark.

Keyhole   Small hole at top of some limpet snails.

Ligament   An internal or external horny band, usually behind the *beaks*, holding the clam's *valves* together or ajar.
Lira(ae)   Fine, raised lines or teeth, usually spiral in nature.
Lunule   A long or heart-shaped impression on the upper margin of the *valves* in front of the clam's *beaks*, one half being in each valve.

Mantle   Soft, fleshy organ producing shelly material..
Millepore growths   Hard encrusting colonies of fire coral.
Multispiral   Of many *whorls*, as in some *opercula*.

Nuclear whorl   The first and smallest *whorl* in the *apex*.
Nucleus   The center or beginning point, usually in an *operculum* or *spire*.

Operculum(opercula)   A 'trapdoor' attached to the foot of a snail that, when withdrawn, helps to seal the *aperture*.
Outer lip   Final edge of the body *whorl*, often thickened in adults.
Ovate   Oval-shaped.

Pallial line   A scar line on the inside of a clam's shell, where the *mantle* muscles are attached.
Pallial sinus   An embayment in the *pallial line* indicating where the *siphon*-retracting muscles are attached to the shell.

Parietal wall   The area on the body *whorl* on the *columella* side of the *aperture* (or *inner lip*).
Paucispiral   Having few *whorls*, as in *Littorina* opercula.
Pelagic   Living or occurring in the upper waters of the ocean.
Periostracum   The *chitinous* layer covering the outer shell, sometimes thin, thick or hairy.
Plankton   Small animals and plants normally floating in the open ocean.
Prodissoconch   Minute, first-formed shell on the clam's *beak*.

Radial   Sculpturing or color rays (in *bivalves*) or ribs (in *univalves*) running parallel to the main *axis*, from *suture* to suture.
Resilium   A horny, pad-like cushion located on the *bivalve's chondrophore*.
Reticulations   Squarish pattern formed by the crossing of concentric and axial sculpturing.

Sculpture   Relief pattern on the shell surface; ribs, spines.
Sinistral   "Left-handed" or of *whorls* growing anti-clockwise.
Siphon   Tube-like extension for passage of water.
Siphonal end   Narrow front end of a shell where the siphon is located.
Spiral   Sculpturing or coloring encircling the *whorls* parallel to the *sutures*.
Spire   The *whorls* at the apical end, exclusive of the last whorl.
Substrate   The bottom or supporting surface.
Subtidal   Below the low tide mark.
Suture   Continuous line on the shell surface where *whorls* adjoin.

Teeth, cardinal   The largest two or three teeth just under the *beak* of a clam.
Teeth, lateral   Smaller, narrow and longer teeth in front or in back of the *cardinal teeth*.

Umbilicus   A central cavity at the base of the shell, around which the *whorls* coil.
Umbo(Umbones)   The *beak* or beginning part of a *bivalve*.
Univalve   A mollusc shell having a single piece (a *gastropod*).

Valve   One of the main shelly halves of a *bivalve*.
Varix   An axial rib or swelling made during a major growth stoppage.

Whorl   A turn or coil of a snail shell.

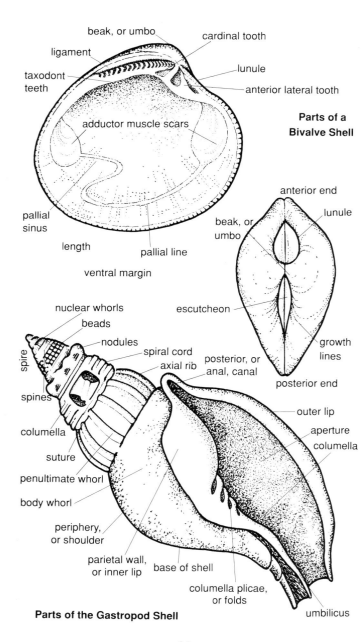

beak, or umbo

cardinal tooth

ligament

lunule

taxodont teeth

anterior lateral tooth

Parts of a Bivalve Shell

adductor muscle scars

pallial sinus

length

pallial line

ventral margin

anterior end

lunule

beak, or umbo

escutcheon

growth lines

posterior end

nuclear whorls

beads

nodules

spiral cord

axial rib

posterior, or anal, canal

spire

spines

outer lip

aperture

columella

columella

suture

penultimate whorl

body whorl

periphery, or shoulder

parietal wall, or inner lip

base of shell

columella plicae, or folds

umbilicus

Parts of the Gastropod Shell

14

THE
PRIMITIVE
SNAILS

Abalones; Ormers
(*Family Haliotidae*)

Worldwide in distribution, the several dozen species of abalones, or ormers as they are called in Europe, are a popular food. The low shell with a large expanded last whorl is characterized by a vivid, iridescent, mother-of-pearl interior and by a series of small, round open holes that help in water circulation. All species live on rocks where encrusting algae are their main source of food.

Black Abalone, *Haliotis cracherodii* Leach, 1814. Shape usually oval, fairly deep, with a smooth outer surface, except for coarse growth lines. Exterior bluish to greenish black. Interior pearly white. About eight or nine holes open, but rarely in freaks they may be absent. This species is uncommon in Oregon, but more common in California where it occurs in crevices in intertidal rocks. The legal capture size is 5 in (12 cm) or more.

Black Abalone
6 in (15 cm)

Red Abalone, *Haliotis rufescens* Swainson, 1822. Oval, rather flattened. Outer surface rough, dull brick-red with a narrow red border around the inner edge of the shell. Interior bright, iridescent blue and greens, with a large central muscle scar. Usually only three or four holes are open. Its main range is from Oregon to central California.

Red Abalone
10 in (26 cm)

Northern Green Abalone,
Haliotis walallensis Stearns, 1899.
Oval-elongate, flattened, with
numerous, small spiral threads.
Exterior dark, brick-red, mottled
with pale green. Moderately
common from British Columbia to
northern California.

Northern Green Abalone
5 in (12.5 cm)

Japanese Abalone, *Haliotis
kamtschatkana* Jonas, 1845.
Elongate, with a moderately high
spire. Usually four or five holes
open which have raised edges.
Exterior of shell roughly
corrugated, but a few specimens
may have weak, spiral threads or
cords. The soft parts are mottled
tan and greenish, but some are
tinged with orange. Tentacles
green and slender. Moderately
common in its northern range
which is from Oregon to southern
Alaska and Japan. Lives on
subtidal rocks.

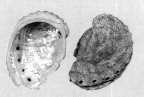

Japanese Abalone
4 in (10 cm)

European Ormer, *Haliotis
tuberculata* Linnaeus, 1758. Shell
elongate, with three or four rapidly
expanding whorls. Exterior
somewhat rough, with growth lines
and fine spiral threads. Dark
reddish brown or mottled in green.
About nine or ten holes open.
Interior bright, whitish, iridescent.
Tentacles on head are long; eyes
bluish. Uncommon on intertidal
rocks in the Channel Islands, but
commoner further south to the
Mediterranean in 3 to 160 ft (1–
50 m). A popular, edible species.

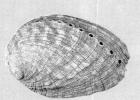

European Ormer
2.5 in (6.5 cm)

Crass Emarginula, *Emarginula
crassa* Sowerby, 1813, is one of
several, small slit limpets belonging
to the family Fissurellidae that live

on subtidal rocks throughout the temperate regions. The small white shells are coiled in their young stages, but grow into shield-shaped limpets. The narrow slit on the back edge of the shell serves as an exodus for water and waste products. This one-inch, white species is distributed from Norway and Iceland to Ireland and Scotland. Sculpture of fine reticulations and with about fifty fine, radiating threads. Fairly common, especially in the north, under stones in subtidal regions to depths of 655 ft (200 m).

Crass Emarginula
1 in (2.5 cm)

Puncturellas and Keyhole Limpets (*Family Fissurellidae*)

These small, usually white limpets have a slot-like opening just in back of the hooked apex. Within the slot is a cup-like shelf. There are about sixty worldwide, mainly deepwater species. Most are believed to feed on sponges.

Hooded Puncturella, *Puncturella cucullata* (Gould, 1846) is a strong, fairly high shell with a small, elevated apex which is hooked over towards the front end. Behind it is a small, elongate slit penetrating through the shell. Exterior of shell with fourteen to twenty-three major radiating ribs with one to five smaller ones between. Fairly common from low

Hooded Puncturella
1 in (2.5 cm)

tide mark to 655 ft (200 m) from Alaska to northern California.

Helmet Puncturella, *Puncturella galeata* (Gould, 1846). Shell solid, fairly high, oval in outline with the larger, posterior half being slightly wider. Slit short and narrow. Ribs numerous, small and of irregular strengths. Exterior gray to whitish; interior glossy white. Lives in rocky and muddy areas from 100 to 490 ft (30–150 m). Moderately common from the Aleutian Islands to northern California coast.

Helmet Puncturella
0.7 in (2 cm)

Volcano Limpet, *Fissurella volcano* Reeve, 1849. Elongate-oval, fairly high shell with a single, oblong hole at the central apex. Sculpture of numerous, rather large, but low and rounded, radial ribs of varying sizes. Exterior gray, with pinkish mauve, radial rays. Interior glossy-white, with a pink line around the callus surrounding the hole. Common on intertidal rocky rubble; uncommon in Oregon, but more common further south to California.

Volcano Limpet
1 in (2.5 cm)

Cloudy Keyhole Limpet, *Fissurella nubecula* (Linnaeus, 1758). Ovate-elongate, fairly high and solid. Exterior with numerous, unequal radial riblets; gray with a dozen rays of dull-purple. Keyhole oblong, parallel-sided. Interior white and green-tinted. The internal callus around the keyhole is white or green and bounded by a brown line. A southern Mediterranean species living as far north as Portugal and southern France. Fairly common on subtidal rocks where it feeds on minute algae.

Cloudy Keyhole Limpet
1 in (2.5 cm)

Graecian Keyhole Limpet,
Diodora graeca (Linnaeus, 1758).
Shell oval, a little narrower in
front. Keyhole is small, oval and
located nearer the front end.
Exterior with numerous, elevated,
radiating ribs, alternately larger
and smaller, with concentric
thread intersecting to form small
square pits. Color dull yellow-
brown, sometimes rayed with
darker brown. Interior white, its
margin strongly denticulate. Callus
around the keyhole is squared off
and minutely excavated behind.
Feeds on sponges. Moderately
common subtidally to 820 ft
(250 m) on rocks. Southern coasts
of the British Isles to the
Mediterranean.

Graecian Keyhole Limpet
0.8 in (2.2 cm)

Italian Keyhole Limpet, *Diodora
italica* (Defrance, 1820). Shell
ovate, narrower in front, rather
depressed; sides are slightly convex
near the edge of the shell, but
concave or straight near the small
keyhole opening. Exterior with
numerous, slightly rounded radial
riblets of unequal size, crossed by
very fine, concentric threads.
Color grayish yellow or solid gray;
sometimes with darker purplish
rays. Moderately common from
Portugal to the Mediterranean on
subtidal rocks.

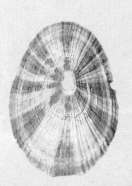

Italian Keyhole Limpet
1.5 in (4 cm)

Rough Keyhole Limpet, *Diodora
aspera* (Rathke, 1833). Shell ovate,
slightly narrower in the front;
moderately elevated. The flat-
sided keyhole is almost round and
located slightly towards the front.
Exterior of rough, radial and
numerous, weaker concentric
threads. Color grayish white with

about twelve to eighteen irregularly sized, purplish blue radial color bands. Interior bluish white; callus around the keyhole is truncated at the front end. It is commonly found attached to rocks from the low tide mark to several feet in depth. Ranges from Cook's Inlet, Alaska, southward to southern California.

Rough Keyhole Limpet
1.5 in (4 cm)

Two-spotted Keyhole Limpet, *Megatebennus bimaculatus* (Dall, 1871). Elongate-oblong, low, with the ends turned up slightly. Large apical keyhole is elongate-oblong, located at the center of the shell. Numerous radial and concentric threads give the exterior a cancellate sculpturing. Brownish to gray with a wide, darker ray on each side. Interior glossy-white. Ranges from Alaska to southern California; common.

Two-spotted Keyhole Limpet
0.7 in (2 cm)

Blue-rayed Limpet, *Helcion pellucidum* (Linnaeus, 1758). Belonging to the following family, Patellidae, this common European species lives on the kelp weed, *Laminaria*. Cap-shaped, sometimes elevated, and has no keyhole or marginal slit. Surface smooth, shiny, horn-colored with narrow, bright-blue rays. No operculum present. The white body has a large head with two tentacles, each bearing an eye at the base. Mantle edge with minute tentacles. This species breeds in winter and in the spring the planktonic young settle on fucoid seaweeds, and later move to kelp. Common subtidally from Norway to Portugal.

Blue-rayed Limpet
0.5 in (1.2 cm)

True Limpets
(*Family Patellidae*)

Several unrelated families produce limpet-shaped shells, but the true limpets are represented by the common, rock-dwelling genus *Patella* in Europe and South Africa. They differ from the similar-looking Acmaeidae of the Americas in lacking leaf-like gill plumes and in having only a gill cordon. No operculum present. Patellids are usually shallow-water rock-dwellers whose shells are greatly influenced by the environment. They are very common in Western Europe but absent in the cooler waters of North America.

Common European Limpet, *Patella vulgata* Linnaeus, 1758. Shell solid, oval and raised; exterior with numerous, irregular small riblets, between which may be smaller radial threads. Growth lines sometimes evident. Color varying from whitish to yellowish, and rarely streaked with dark-brown. Interior weakly iridescent, the center clouded with a whitish callus. A common, edible, rock-dwelling species living from Norway to the Mediterranean.

Limpets that live in the upper tidal region are usually higher in outline than those living closer to the constant impact of incoming waves.

Low and high form of Common European Limpet
2 in (5 cm)

European China Limpet, *Patella aspera* Röding, 1798. Similar to the Common European Limpet, but more elongate. Exterior with strong, sharper ribs, resulting in a serrated edge to the shell. Interior porcellaneous white, with a head scar of pale-orange. Common from the southern British Isles to southern France.

Common China Limpet
1.5 in (4 cm)

✦

American Limpets
(*Families Acmaeidae and Lottiidae*)

The western coast of North America abounds with a variety of limpets, many formerly placed in the genus *Collisella* (now *Lottia*). The family Acmaeidae includes the single, white-shelled limpet of the Pacific coast of North America and a few blind, small deep-sea pectinodont limpets. The remaining nineteen species of *Lottia* and *Tectura* belong to the family Lottiidae.

White-cap Limpet, *Acmaea mitra* Rathke, 1833. Shell white or grayish white, solid, conic in shape

with an almost circular base. Apex
pointed and near the center. Often
covered with small knobby millepore
growths. Interior white. Edge of shell
smooth. Rarely pink-rayed. Most
abundant in its northern range from
the Aleutian Islands, but uncommon
as far south as southern California.

Shield Limpet, *Lottia pelta*
(Rathke, 1833). Shell strong, base
elliptical in outline, with a
moderately high apex situated
almost near the center. Exterior
has about twenty-five very weak,
radial riblets. Color cream-gray
with strong black radial, often
intertwining, stripes. Inner border
edge with alternating black and
cream bars. A common intertidal
rock-dweller from Alaska to
Mexico.

White-cap Limpet
1 in (2.5 cm)

File Limpet, *Lottia limatula*
(Carpenter 1864). Base elliptical
to almost round; low to quite flat.
Characterized by radial rows of
small beads which form tiny
riblets. Exterior greenish black.
Interior glossy white with bluish
tint. Edge of shell usually has a
solid, black-brown, narrow color
band. A common intertidal, rock
species occurring from Puget
Sound, Washington, south to
southern California.

Shield Limpet
1.2 in (3 cm)

Fingered Limpet, *Lottia digitalis*
(Rathke, 1833). Elliptical to ovate
in outline; with a moderately high
apex minutely hooked forward and
placed one third back from the
front edge. With fifteen to twenty-
five moderately well-developed,
coarse radial ribs which give the

File Limpet
1.2 in (3 cm)

shell a wavy border. Color grayish with tiny, distinct mottlings of white dots and blackish streaks and lines. Interior white with a faint bluish tint and with a large, usually even, head patch of dark-brown in the center. Inner edge of shell with a solid or broken, narrow band of black-brown. A common species preferring vertical rock surfaces where action is severe. A homing species ranging from the Aleutians to California.

Fingered Limpet
1 in (2.5 cm)

Unstable Limpet, *Lottia instabilis* (Gould, 1846). A small, solid, all-brown species living on the stems of large kelp weeds. Shell heavy, oblong, with a high spire, and with its sides compressed. Lower edge curved so that the shell may fit evenly against its kelp stem substrate. Exterior smoothish, a dull light-brown. Interior whitish with a faint brown stain in the center and with a narrow, solid border of brown. Moderately common from Alaska to southern California.

Unstable Limpet
1 in (2.5 cm)

Mask Limpet, *Tectura persona* (Rathke, 1833). Oval-elongate, smoothish, with a fairly high apex pointing forward and one third the way back from the front edge. Exterior smoothish with a fine pattern of white squares and triangles on a dark-gray background. Interior bluish white to blackish blue. This species is very common from northern California to Alaska where it lives between tides on rocks where strong waves flush the shaded rock crevices.

Mask Limpet
1.2 in (3 cm)

Pacific Plate Limpet, *Tectura scutum* (Rathke, 1833). Shell fairly large, almost round in outline, quite flat, with the apex towards the center of the shell. Smoothish, except for very fine radial riblets, seen best in young specimens. Exterior greenish gray, with slate-gray radial bands or mottlings. Interior bluish white with faint or darkish brown head scar. Inner edge with alternating, small bars of blackish brown and bluish white. A rock-dweller along the coasts of Alaska to Oregon where it is common; in California it is rare.

A similar species, *Tectura tessulata* (Müller, 1776) from the British Isles is only 0.5 in (15 mm) narrower at the front end and has chocolate-brown radial patterns. It is locally called the Tortoiseshell Limpet and is common in rocky tidepools.

Pacific Plate Limpet
1.5 in (4 cm)

Rough Pacific Limpet, *Tectura scabra* (Gould, 1846). Elliptical in outline, with a fairly low apex located one third back from the front end. The fifteen to twenty-five strong, coarse radiating ribs make the edge wavy. Color a dirty gray-green. Interior glossy, whitish and irregularly stained in the center with brown. Edge of the shell between the serrations stained with purplish brown. A common species found clinging to gently sloping rock surfaces. It is a southern species ranging from Oregon to Baja California.

Rough Pacific Limpet
1 in (2.5 cm)

Seaweed Limpet, *Discurria insessa* (Hinds, 1842). A small, solid shell, with a high spire and compressed, parallel sides. Twice as long as wide. Exterior a uniform, greasy light-brown. Abundant on the stalks and holdfasts of the large kelps, such as *Egregia*. Occurs along the Pacific coast from Alaska to Baja California.

Seaweed Limpet
0.6 in (1.5 cm)

Trochoid Snails
(*Family Trochidae*)

This is a very diversified snail family, of many genera and species, found in most parts of the world, from intertidal habitats to very deep water. Most have an iridescent, mother-of-pearl finish inside the top-shaped shell. The operculum is circular, of many whorls and corneous.

Greenland Margarite,
Margarites groenlandicus (Gmelin, 1791). Shell small, trochoid in shape, with the angle of the spire about 110°. Whorls strongly rounded, aperture round, umbilicus wide and deep. Outer lip and columella very thin. Base smooth; top of whorls glassy-smooth. Suture is finely impressed. Color glossy-cream. Common on sandy and rock bottoms from 30 to 985 ft (10–300 m) from the Arctic Seas to Maine and to the British Isles.

Greenland Margarite
0.5 in (1.2 cm)

Northern Rosy Margarite,
Margarites costalis (Gould, 1841).
Shell a little wider than high and
with five evenly and well-rounded
whorls. Narrowly and deeply
umbilicate. Angle of spire about
90°. Next to last whorl with two to
four unequal, raised spiral cords.
Base with eight to ten threads.
Color rosy to grayish cream. White
within the smooth umbilicus.
Aperture pearly-rose. Common
from Greenland to Massachusetts;
and from Alaska.

Northern Rosy Margarite
0.5 in (1.2 cm)

Sordid Margarite, *Margarites
sordidus* (Hancock, 1846). Shell
very similar to *M. costalis*, but
usually larger, with more rounded
whorls, finer spiral, uneven
threads, and with numerous, very
fine, slanting, axial threads. Suture
more strongly indented, below
which are crowded, short, slanting
riblets. This species is found in
Arctic waters around the world.

Sordid Margarite
0.8 in (2 cm)

Puppet Margarite, *Margarites
pupillus* (Gould, 1849). Trochoid
in shape. Five or six whorls, the
upper ones with five or six
smoothish, small, spiral threads
between or over which are
microscopic, axial, slanting
threads. Umbilicus narrow and
deep. Exterior a dull, chalky-white
to yellowish gray. Aperture rosy to
greenish pearl. A common littoral
species from Alaska to Oregon.

Puppet Margarite
0.4 in (1 cm)

Lovely Pacific Solarelle,
Solariella permabilis Carpenter,
1864. Shell small, as long as wide,
solid, semi-glossy. Umbilicus fairly
wide, round, very deep and

bordered by a strong beaded cord. Seven whorls, shouldered just below the suture by a flat shelf. Color tan with light-mauve streaks and mottlings. Moderately common on rocky rubble bottoms from 330 to 1970 ft (100–600 m). Japan and Alaska south to off California.

Lovely Pacific Solarelle
0.7 in (2 cm)

Obscure Solarelle, *Solariella obscura* (Couthouy, 1838). Shell small; whorls strongly shouldered by one or two large, feebly beaded, spiral cords above the periphery. Base smoothish, except for microscopic spiral scratches. Umbilicus narrow and bordered by an angular rim. Color grayish to pinkish tan, often eroded to reveal a pearly-golden color. Commonly dredged from 20 to 2,600 ft (6–800 m) from the Arctic Seas to Virginia and from Alaska to Washington; also Norway.

Obscure Solarelle
0.4 in (1 cm)

Otto's Spiny Margarite, *Lischkeia ottoi* (Philippi, 1844). Shell small, lightweight, as wide as long. Exterior pearly-white. Sculpture of whorls in the spire with three evenly spaced, spiral rows of prickly beads. Nuclear whorls with axial riblets. Nova Scotia to off North Carolina and from Norway to off France.

Otto's Spiny Margarite
0.7 in (2 cm)

Regular Spiny Margarite, *Lischkeia regularis* (Verrill and Smith, 1880). Similar to *L. ottoi*, but the umbilicus is nearly closed, the whorls are more rounded and well-beaded by three or four prominent spiral rows of tiny, sharp beads. The base has five spiral threads bearing minute

Regular Spiny Margarite
0.7 in (2 cm)

beads. Color grayish, dull-white. Fairly common offshore from Nova Scotia to off New York.

Adams' Spiny Margarite, *Lischkeia cidaris* (Carpenter, 1864). Shell moderately fragile, sculptured with three or four spiral rows of fairly large beads. Suture deeply indented. Base with seven or eight smaller, weakly beaded, spiral cords. Outer lip thin and wavy. Exterior grayish tan. Operculum thin, translucent brown, multispiral. Moderately common offshore from Alaska to southern California.

Adams' Spiny Margarite
1.5 in (4 cm)

Northern Top-shell, *Calliostoma occidentale* (Mighels and Adams, 1842). Shell small, trochoid, glistening iridescent white. Whorls convex and with three or four strong spiral cords, the lower ones smooth, the uppermost neatly beaded. No umbilicus. Outer lip fragile, slightly crenulated. Interior pearly white. Spire straight-sided, sometimes with a reddish tinge. Common from Nova Scotia to off New Jersey; Scandinavia and Iceland to northern British Isles.

Northern Top-shell
0.5 in (1.2 cm)

Baird's Top-shell, *Calliostoma bairdii* Verrill and Smith, 1880. Shell solid, with straight sides and an apical angle of about 70°. Base rather flat, periphery of the last whorl strongly angular. Sculpture of six or seven spiral rows of small, neat beads. No umbilicus. Color brownish cream with faint maculations of iridescent reddish. Moderately common offshore from New England to northeastern Florida.

Baird's Top-shell
1 in (2.5 cm)

Ringed Top-shell, *Calliostoma annulatum* (Lightfoot, 1786). An unusually beautiful shell, trochoid in shape, with a flattish spire at an angle of about 70°. Lightweight, golden-yellow in background color with a mauve band at the periphery of the whorls. Has numerous spiral rows of tiny, distinct beads, usually five to eight rows in the spire whorls. Nucleus pink. No umbilicus. Outer lip sharp and finely crenulated. Operculum corneous, circular and light-yellow. Ranges from southern Alaska to northern Baja California.

Ringed Top-shell
1 in (2.5 cm)

Channeled Top-shell, *Calliostoma canaliculatum* (Lightfoot, 1786). Shell lightweight, spire sharp and with straight sides. Periphery of last whorl rather sharp and angular. Base of shell almost flat. The numerous sharp spiral cords are slightly beaded and make the suture between whorls difficult to distinguish. Nuclear whorls white. Fairly common on kelps. Ranges from Alaska to southern California.

Channeled Top-shell
1.5 in (4 cm)

Western Ribbed Top-shell, *Calliostoma ligatum* (Gould, 1849). Shell solid and rather heavy, with well-rounded whorls. Six to eight strong, smooth spiral, light-brown cords on a background of dark-chocolate. Rarely flushed with mauve. No umbilicus. Aperture pearly white. A very common littoral species from Alaska to northern California, but rare southward.

Western Ribbed Top-shell
0.8 in (2 cm)

Variable Top-shell, *Calliostoma variegatum* (Carpenter, 1864). Shell solid, its spire slightly concave and the indented sutures quite prominent. Periphery of the last whorl well-rounded. Five or six beaded cords on the above whorls. Nucleus pinkish. Color light-tan with speckles of reddish brown. Ranges from Alaska to southern California.

Variable Top-shell
1 in (2.5 cm)

European Painted Top-shell, *Calliostoma zizyphinus* Linnaeus, 1758. Solid, trochoid in shape, with a flat-sided apex with an angle of about 70°. Periphery on last whorl well-rounded. Whorls with three to five spiral, smooth cords, the largest being just above the suture. Color pale-yellow with streaks and blotches of darker tan. Umbilicus slightly indented. Ranges from Norway to the Mediterranean.

European Painted Top-shell
1 in (2.5 cm)

European Granular Top-shell, *Calliostoma granulatum* (Born, 1778). Spire pointed, slightly concave. Whorls above have six or seven smaller, beaded spiral threads. Suture minutely indented. Base of shell with a dozen faint spiral threads and colored cream with numerous reddish brown spots. Uncommon from 23 to 985 ft (7–300 m) on rough, stony bottoms. Ranges from the southern British Isles to the Azores and Mediterranean.

European Granular Top-shell
1 in (2.5 cm)

Gualteri's Top-shell, *Calliostoma gualterianum* (Philippi, 1848). Shell conical-elevated, without an umbilicus, polished, solid, yellowish brown or olive, clouded with dark-brown, the earlier whorls bluish black. Colors variable, and rarely all purple. A common shallow-water species ranging from Portugal, south into the Mediterranean.

Exasperating Top-shell, *Jujubinus exasperatus* (Pennant, 1777). Shell small, solid, pyramidal with a high spire and flat sides. Sculpture of three or four large, rounded, coarsely beaded cords. Base with six flattish, smooth cords. Umbilicus absent. Color of variable maculations of reds, browns and tans. Fairly common from southern England south into the Mediterranean.

Black Tegula, *Tegula funebralis* (A. Adams, 1855). Heavy, solid, dark purple-black in color; smoothish, but with a narrow, puckered band just below the suture. Weak spiral cords rarely evident; coarse growth lines present in large, more elongate specimens. Base rounded. Umbilicus closed or merely a slight dimple. Columella pearly, with two small nodules at the base. The head and tentacles are entirely black. The sole of the foot of males is usually light-cream in color, that of the females usually brownish. A very common littoral, rock-dwelling species ranging from Vancouver, Canada, to southern California.

Magical Gibbula, *Gibbula magus* (Linnaeus, 1758). Shell solid, low-spired, with shouldered whorls bearing coarse nodules just below

Gualteri's Top-shell
0.5 in (1.2 cm)

Exasperating Top-shell
0.4 in (10 cm)

Black Tegula
1.5 in (4 cm)

the suture. Last whorl keeled and smooth. Umbilicus small. Base with fine spiral lines. Last whorl with irregular, slanting axial swellings. Columella thin, white, with a bulge in the center. Color variable browns and reddish maculations. Animal yellowish pink with blackish purple blotches. A subtidal species in southern British Isles and south into the Mediterranean.

Magical Gibbula
2 in (3 cm)

Ashen Gibbula, *Gibbula cineraria* (Linnaeus, 1758). Shell solid, somewhat dome-shaped with a slightly convex spire and blunt apex. Sculpture of numerous, low, slightly nodulose, spiral ridges crossed by fine growth lines. Umbilicus narrow but deep. Color yellowish with numerous broken, slanting streaks of brownish purple. A very common intertidal species on rocky shores among weeds and under stones. Found throughout the British Isles and from Iceland to Portugal.

Ashen Gibbula
0.8 in (2 cm)

Umbilicate Gibbula, *Gibbula umbilicalis* (da Costa, 1778). Shell solid, somewhat globular, with a convex, rounded spire and flat apex. Surface smoothish, except for fine, incised lines and eight to ten grooves on the base. Umbilicus fairly large and deep. Color heavily maculated with speckles of reddish brown on a cream background; sometimes with axial, slanting flames of red-brown. A common intertidal species found among weeds and stones in tidepools. Eggs are laid singly and fertilized externally by floating sperm.

Umbilicate Gibbula
0.8 in (2 cm)

Ranges from the southern British Isles to the Mediterranean.

Lined Monodont, *Monodonta lineata* (da Costa, 1778). Shell globose, large, heavy, with somewhat rounded whorls. Surface smoothish to rough with low, weak, spiral ridges. Irregular growth lines are frequent. Color dark-gray with a fine mottled pattern and a large white area surrounding the indented umbilical area. Columella with a swollen, small tooth near the base. The animal is grayish green with numerous black lines. A fairly common rock pool-dweller, feeding on vegetable detritus and soft algae. Ranges from the southern British Isles to Portugal.

Lined Monodont
1.2 in (3 cm)

Articulate Monodont, *Monodonta articulata* Lamarck, 1822. Shell solid, trochoid in shape, with a rounded spire. Umbilicus absent. Surface rough. Color gray-green or dirty white, with numerous spiral bands of alternating squares of white and reddish brown. Some specimens are conspicuously spirally grooved, some quite smooth. A common southern littoral snail ranging from southern France and Portugal to the Mediterranean.

Articulate Monodont
1 in (2.5 cm)

✦

THE
ADVANCED
SHELLS

Periwinkles
(*Family Littorinidae*)

Throughout most parts of the world the small periwinkles appear in large numbers along rocky shores between tide marks or on wharf pilings and mangrove trees. They feed on vegetable detritus and living algae.

Common Periwinkle, *Littorina littorea* (Linnaeus, 1758). Shell globular, solid, with a coarse exterior and a strong, thin outer lip. Columella arched, smooth and white. Sculpture of faint spiral lines. Color drab grayish, sometimes with fine, spiral streaks of whitish. This species is common on intertidal rocks in exposed areas. It ranges from Greenland and Norway to the Mediterranean; and from northern Canada to Delaware.

Common Periwinkle
1 in (2.5 cm)

Marsh Periwinkle, *Littorina irrorata* (Say, 1822). Thick-shelled, with numerous, regularly formed, spiral grooves. Outer lip slightly flaring and with tiny grooves on the inside. Color grayish, with tiny, short streaks of reddish brown on the spiral ridges. Aperture yellowish. Columella reddish brown. Commonly found in large numbers among the sedges of brackish water marshes. Ranges from New York to central Florida and to Texas.

Marsh Periwinkle
1 in (2.5 cm)

Northern Yellow Periwinkle, *Littorina obtusata* (Linnaeus, 1758). Small, globular, solid, with a low spire and smoothish exterior. Color variable but usually a uniform bright brownish yellow or orange-yellow. Operculum yellowish or brownish. It is a common rocky coast species, found from southern Labrador to New Jersey; Norway to the Mediterranean.

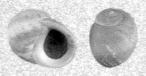

Northern Yellow Periwinkle
0.5 in (1.2 cm)

Northern Rough Periwinkle, *Littorina saxatilis* (Olivi, 1792). Shell solid, with a pointed spire, rather distinctly rounded whorls and an impressed suture. Surface smoothish, except for numerous, indistinct spiral threads which are usually sharply sloping in cross-section. Typical form gray with a darker tessellate pattern and a dark aperture. The form (or another species) *rudis* Maton, 1797, lacks the tessellate pattern, has a broader lower columella and the aperture is light-colored. A moderately common, high intertidal, rock species. It lives in the Arctic Seas south to New Jersey; south to Puget Sound, Washington; and south from Norway to France.

Northern Rough Periwinkle
0.5 in (1.2 cm)

Eroded Periwinkle, *Littorina keenae* Rosewater, 1978. Shell small, with a pointed spire, usually badly eroded. Color grayish brown with bluish white spots and flecks. There is a flattened, eroded area on the body whorl alongside the whitish columella. Interior of aperture chocolate-brown with a white spiral band at the bottom. An abundant species on rocky

Eroded Periwinkle
0.7 in (2 cm)

shore flats in the splash zone. Found from Puget Sound, Washington, to Mexico. Formerly called *Littorina planaxis* Philippi.

Checkered Periwinkle, *Littorina scutulata* Gould, 1849. Shell small, somewhat elongate, with a pointed spire. The columella is not as broad as that in the Eroded Periwinkle. Surface smooth, semi-glossy. Color light to dark reddish brown, and often with fairly large, irregular spots and blotches of bluish white. Common in the upper intertidal zone. Distributed from Kodiak Island, Alaska, south to the northwestern part of Baja California, Mexico.

Checkered Periwinkle
0.5 in (1.2 cm)

Purple Sea-snails and Turret-shells
(*Families Janthinidae and Turritellidae*)

The purple sea-snails are a small family of pelagic snails, usually inhabiting the surface of warm seas, but sometimes drifting into colder waters. A float of bubbles is created by the animal, and in some species the egg capsules are attached to the underside. The elongate, narrow, many-whorled turret-shells are mostly warm-water, mud-dwellers with only a few species occurring in cold waters. The operculum is thin, chitinous, circular, with many whorls and often has bristles along the edge.

Common Purple Sea-snail, *Janthina janthina* (Linnaeus, 1758). Whorls angular, two-toned with purplish white on the apex side and deep violet on the umbilical side. Base of columella not extended. Rarely cast ashore in southern New England and the British Isles.

Common Purple Sea-snail
1 in (2.5 cm)

Eroded Turret-shell, *Tachyrhynchus erosus* (Couthouy, 1838). Elongate, eight to ten whorls which have five or six flat-topped, spiral cords. No umbilicus. Aperture round; columella smooth. Color chalky-cream with a polished, tan periostracum. Common from 45 to 460 ft (14–140 m) on mud bottoms. Arctic Seas to off Massachusetts and also south to British Columbia.

Eroded Turret-shell
1 in (2.5 cm)

Common Turret-shell, *Turritella communis* Risso, 1829. Elongate, about fifteen whorls; spire usually eroded. Spiral cords small and numerous. Brownish yellow with the base tinged with lilac. Abundant in muddy, shallow waters from Norway to North Africa.

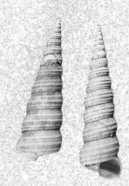

Common Turret-shell
1 in (2.5 cm)

◆

Wentletraps
(*Family Epitoniidae*)

The wentletraps are a popular group of shells noted for their pure-white shells bearing numerous, sharp, axial ribs. The aperture is always round and fitted with a black or brown, chitinous operculum. The white animal feeds on sea-anemones and when disturbed may give off a purple fluid. The family has numerous genera, with shells that are smooth, reticulated or with sharp ribs.

Northern White Wentletrap, *Acirsa borealis* (Lyell, 1842). Elongate, chalky-white to yellowish; surface has very weak, axial riblets, and numerous, spiral cut lines, sometimes filled with thin periostracum. Two nuclear whorls are smooth. Edge of outer lip thin. Uncommon from just offshore down to 330 ft (100 m). Aleutian Islands to Greenland and south to Massachusetts.

Northern White Wentletrap
1 in (2.5 cm)

Costate Wentletrap, *Acirsa costulata* (Mighels and Adams, 1842) is very similar to *A. borealis* and is sometimes considered a synonym. It is much more elongate, the spire angle is much less, the base of the whorls have a weak carina, the surface is smoother and yellowish. Uncommon offshore in New England waters.

Costate Wentletrap
1.2 in (3 cm)

Wroblewski's Wentletrap, *Opalia wroblewskii* (Mörch, 1876).

Elongate, solid, always looks beachworn. Grayish white, but often stained purple from its own dye. Has six to eight low, pronounced axial ribs. Base of shell bounded by a strong, smooth, low spiral cord. Fairly common from 3 to 330 ft (1–100 m) from Alaska to southern California.

Wroblewski's Wentletrap
1 in (2.5 cm)

Money Wentletrap, *Epitonium indianorum* (Carpenter, 1864). Slender, with about ten well-rounded whorls and a deeply indented suture. Each whorl has fourteen or fifteen sharp, axial ribs which are slightly bent backwards. Tops of the ribs are slightly pointed. Fairly common offshore on gravel bottoms associated with sea-anemones. In shallow water from Alaska to British Columbia, but in deeper water further south to Baja California and Mexico.

Money Wentletrap
1 in (2.5 cm)

Greenland Wentletrap, *Epitonium greenlandicum* (Perry, 1811). Solid, elongate, chalky-gray, with nine to twelve ridge-like, sometimes broad, ribs per whorl. Spiral sculpture prominent, with nine spiral cords on base of shell. Operculum dark-brown. Common offshore on gravel bottoms from 65 to 850 ft (20–260 m). Ranges from Alaska to British Columbia and from Greenland to Long Island, New York.

Greenland Wentletrap
1.2 in (3 cm)

Angulate Wentletrap, *Epitonium angulatum* (Say, 1830). Moderately stout, strong and pure-white. Eight whorls with about nine or ten strong, but thin, axial ribs which are very slightly reflected

backwards and which are usually
angulated at the shoulder. The ribs
are usually lined up one below the
other. Outer lip thickened and
reflected. One of the commonest
shallow-water, sand-dwelling
wentletraps ranging from New
York to Florida and to Texas.

Humphrey's Wentletrap,
Epitonium humphreysi (Kiener,
1838). Fairly slender, thick-
shelled, dull-white and with a deep
suture. The nine or ten convex
whorls each have eight or nine ribs
that are slightly angled at the
shoulder. Outer lip round and
thickened. Common from sandy
shores to 330 ft (100 m). Extends
from Massachusetts to Florida and
to Texas.

Brown-banded Wentletrap,
Epitonium rupicola (Kurtz, 1860).
Moderately stout, whitish to
yellowish with two brownish spiral
bands on either side of the deep
suture. Twelve to eighteen weak or
strong riblets on each whorl. A
former, thickened varix is
sometimes present on the whorl
above. Base of shell has a single,
fine spiral cord. Common from
low water to about 130 ft (40 m).
Ranges from Massachusetts to
Florida and to Texas.

**Common European
Wentletrap**, *Epitonium clathrus*
(Linnaeus, 1758). Elongate,
strong; whorls barely meeting but
linked and braced by eight or nine
strong, axial ribs. Behind the thick,
round outer lip there is a swollen
varix. Color grayish yellow; the
ribs spotted with brown spiral

Angulate Wentletrap
1 in (2.5 cm)

Humphrey's Wentletrap
0.8 in (2 cm)

Brown-banded Wentletrap
1 in (2.5 cm)

lines. Animal white with purplish black specks. Common from intertidal sand flats to 230 ft (70 m). Norway to the Mediterranean and Black Sea.

Turton's Wentletrap, *Epitonium turtonis* (Turton, 1819). Similar to *E. clathrus*, but the whorls are more flat-sided, with twelve to fifteen ribs per whorl, the top of the ribs reflected and flattened against the sutures, and is usually more darkly colored. Spaces between ribs with fine, spiral scratches. Moderately common on sandy bottoms from 16 to 65 ft (5–20 m). Ranges from Norway to Portugal.

Trevely's Wentletrap, *Epitonium trevelyanum* (Johnston, 1841). Shell white, moderately elongate, with about fourteen ribs per whorl, the tops being thickened, triangular and flattened. Suture very deep. Spiral lines sometimes present, as well as a peripheral brown, spiral band. Uncommon offshore from Norway to Portugal.

Common European Wentletrap
1.5 in (4 cm)

Turton's Wentletrap
1.5 in (4 cm)

Trevely's Wentletrap
0.8 in (2 cm)

Hairy-shells
(*Family Trichotropidae*)

Members of this cold-water family are characterized by the hairy periostracal layer covering the outer shell. They have a turbinate shell with a short, pointed spire and a fairly large aperture. The operculum is chitinous, with few whorls. In some species, one-year-old snails are males, but turn into females in the second year, and die after laying their gelatinous egg capsules.

Two-keeled Hairy-shell, *Trichotropis bicarinata* (Sowerby, 1825). Shell as wide as tall, with a sharp apex, and about four whorls which have two strong, spiral cords at the periphery. The columella is wide and flattened. The delicate periostracum is brown and very spinose on the shoulders of the whorls. Moderately common offshore. Occurs in Arctic Seas to the Queen Charlotte Islands, British Columbia, and Labrador and Newfoundland.

Two-keeled Hairy-shell
1.5 in (4 cm)

Grey Hairy-shell, *Trichotropis insignis* Middendorff, 1849. Similar to *T. bicarinata* but less than 1 in (2 cm). A heavier shell, weakly carinate, with numerous, uneven spiral threads, and a thin grayish periostracum. Uncommon offshore from Alaska to northern Japan.

Grey Hairy-shell
1 in (2.5 cm)

Cancellate Hairy-shell, *Trichotropis borealis* (Hinds, 1843). Has five or six rounded whorls bearing between sutures four or five strong, spiral cords, between which there may be small, axial riblets which produce a cancellate sculpture. Spire high. Periostracum thick, brown and with bristles over the region of the cords. A common shallow-water species from the Bering Sea to off Oregon.

Cancellate Hairy-shell
0.8 in (2 cm)

Cap Limpets and Chinese Hats
(*Families Capulidae and Crepidulidae*)

The cap limpets begin life as small, coiled shells, but upon settling on a stone or bivalve shell, they grow into a cap-shaped limpet. The proboscis, which is formed from the forefoot, is permanently extended from the mouth and used to gather food or the pseudofeces of its bivalve host.

The chinese hats, or cup-and-saucer shells, are related to the slipper shells but have an extra shelf or cup within the main shell. They lack an operculum and are ciliary feeders, trapping floating food particles on a mucous sheet on the gills.

Fool's Cap Limpet, *Capulus ungaricus* (Linnaeus, 1767). Cap-shaped, with a small hooked apex. Shell strong, yellowish white, with an ashy-brown, shaggy periostracum. Irregularly sculptured with coarse threads. Ranges from Greenland to off northeast Florida; and from Norway and Iceland to Portugal.

Fool's Cap Limpet
1.5 in (4 cm)

Pacific Chinese Hat, *Calyptraea fastigiata* Gould, 1856. Outline of the base of the thin, strong shell is circular and the apex is at the center of the shell. Color white to gray. Moderately common offshore, attached to other shells and to stones. Ranges from Alaska to California.

Pacific Chinese Hat
1 in (2.5 cm)

European Chinese Hat,
Calyptraea chinensis (Linnaeus,
1758). Similar to the Pacific
Chinese Hat; exterior with
concentric, pustulose growth rings.
Common subtidally on other shells
and on stones. Ranges from the
British Isles to Portugal.

European Chinese Hat
0.6 in (1.5 cm)

Slipper-shells
(Family Crepidulidae)

The curious cup inside the cup-and-saucer shells and the broad
shelf within the slipper-shells are for the protection of the soft
digestive gland of the animal. Most species adhere permanently
to other dead shells, with the smaller males usually attached to
the larger females. Males customarily turn into females after the
second or third year. Eggs, laid in soft capsules, are attached to
the substrate under the shell and are brooded until the free-
swimming larval stages emerge.

Striate Cup-and-saucer,
Crucibulum striatum Say, 1824.
Cap-shaped; base circular, with
the slightly twisted, smooth apex
near the center of the shell.
Interior shelly cap two-thirds free
from attachment. Exterior gray,
with small, wavy radial cords.
Commonly dredged offshore from
20 to 650 ft (6–200 m). Found in
the Maritime Provinces of Canada
to off Florida.

Striate Cup-and-saucer
1 in (2.5 cm)

Pacific Half-slipper, *Crepipatella lingulata* (Gould, 1846). Shell small, with an almost circular base; apex near edge of shell. Interior tannish mauve with a small cup attached along one side only. Exterior wrinkled and brownish. Common on living snail shells. Ranges from the Bering Sea to Panama.

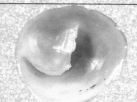

Pacific Half-slipper
0.7 in (2 cm)

Hooked Slipper-shell, *Crepidula adunca* Sowerby, 1825. Highly arched, with a sharp, hooked apex. Laterally compressed, giving a triangular appearance from the sides. Color dark brown with lighter rays and spots. Interior brown. Commonly found on small shells. Ranges from British Columbia to southern California.

Hooked Slipper-shell
1 in (2.5 cm)

European White Slipper-shell, *Crepidula unguiformis* Lamarck, 1822. Shell pure-white, solid, usually quite flat, or concave if attached to the interior aperture of a large gastropod shell. Apex at the end and with small, glossy nuclear whorls. Inner shelf about half the length of the entire shell, glossy-white and slightly concave. Exterior dull-white to dirty-gray. Commonly found on large dead shells. This is a southern species ranging from southern France and Portugal to the Mediterranean.

European White Slipper-shell
1 in (2.5 cm)

Western White Slipper-shell, *Crepidula nummaria* Gould, 1846. Shell elongate, flattened and slightly concave, with a glossy-white underside and a large deck which usually has a weak, raised ridge running from the apical end forward to the leading edge of the shelf. Exterior whitish, usually with a thin, yellowish periostracum. Found in rock crevices and the apertures of dead shells. Extends along the entire west coast from Alaska to Panama, usually in shallow water.

Western white Slipper-shell
1.2 in (3 cm)

Eastern White Slipper-shell, *Crepidula plana* Say, 1822. Shell thin but strong; pure-white. Very flat, sometimes convex or concave depending upon the shape of the substrate. The glossy-white shelf is smooth and somewhat convex. The apex is rarely turned to one side. Several specimens customarily congregate on dead shells or horseshoe crabs, *Limulus*, with the larger ones being females and the smaller, surrounding ones being males. When the female dies or is removed, the nearest male gradually turns into a female. The egg capsules are brooded under the front of the foot of the female. Slipper-shells are diatom filter feeders. This very common species extends from eastern Canada to Texas and south to Brazil.

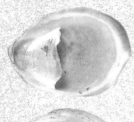

Eastern White Slipper-shell
1.2 in (3 cm)

Convex Slipper-shell, *Crepidula convexa* Say, 1822. Shell small, usually highly arched and colored a dark reddish to purplish brown. Some specimens may be spotted. The edge of the deck is almost straight. There is a small muscle scar inside the main shell on the right side just under the outer corner of the deck. Most live on other dead shells, but sometimes they settle on eelgrass where specimens become long and narrow. Occurs from Massachusetts to Texas and the

Convex Slipper-shell
0.5 in (1.2 cm)

West Indies. Introduced to California prior to 1899.

Common Atlantic Slipper-shell, *Crepidula fornicata* (Linnaeus, 1758). Shelly deck extends over the rear half of the inside of the arched shell. The deck is usually slightly concave and white to buff; its edge is strongly sinuate or waved in two places. Exterior dirty-white to tan, sometimes with brown blotches and lines. Variable in shape. They may be strongly corrugated if living on a ribbed scallop. This common, shallow-water species has been introduced to northwestern America and western Europe. Its normal range is from the Maritime Provinces of Canada to Texas.

Common Atlantic Slipper-shell
1.5 in (4 cm)

White Hoof-shell, *Hipponix antiquatus* (Linnaeus, 1767). Small, heavy for its size, cap-shaped, with a poorly developed spire. Nuclear whorls minute, spiral and glossy-white. There is a horseshoe-shaped muscle scar inside the shell. Exterior with prominent, rugose ribs crossed by incised lines. Periostracum thin, light-yellow. Sometimes with strong, smooth, circular cords. No operculum. Belongs to the family Hipponicidae. Found intertidally under stones or on other shells from British Columbia to Peru; and from Florida to Brazil.

White Hoof-shell
0.5 in (1.2 cm)

◆

Lamellaria and Velutina Snails
(*Families Lamellariidae and Velutinidae*)

The lamellarian snails have very thin, fragile shells that are buried in a large, slug-like animal. They are associated with shallow-water, compound ascidians upon which they feed and lay their eggs. They are hermaphroditic, with all individuals bearing a short, prong-like penis.

Transparent Lamellaria, *Lamellaria perspicua* (Linnaeus, 1758). Shell fragile, smooth, transparent, almost without growth lines, and with two whorls. Nuclear whorl is slightly elevated. Columella slit open, so apex can be seen from below. Operculum absent. Uncommon in rock pools down to 330 ft (100 m). Occurs from Norway and Iceland to the Mediterranean; eastern United States to Florida and to Brazil.

Transparent Lamellaria
0.5 in (1.2 cm)

Smooth Velutina, *Velutina velutina* (Müller, 1776). Shell very thin, fragile, translucent-amber, and covered with a thick, brownish periostracum which is spirally ridged. Columella arched and narrow. Found in the low tide area on rocky shores where it feeds on solitary ascidians. This is a circumboreal species extending south to the British Isles, California and to Massachusetts.

Smooth Velutina
0.7 in (1.7 cm)

False Arctic Slipper-shell,
Capulacmaea commodum
(Middendorff, 1851). A thin-
shelled, white, cap-shaped shell
covered with a thin brown
periostracum. The shell is
sometimes strongly rayed near the
anterior end. This cold-water
species is in the family Velutinidae,
and has a wide distribution in
circumpolar waters.

False Arctic Slipper-shell
1 in (2.5 cm)

Pelican
Foot Shells
(*Family Aporrhaidae*)

In what was once a widely distributed and diverse family of
snails, less than a half-dozen now survive in the northern
Atlantic. The outer lip of the shell is expanded into the shape of
a webbed foot of a bird. They are detritus feeders that live on
muddy bottoms. The foot is elongate and bears a long, narrow,
chitinous operculum.

American Pelican's Foot,
Aporrhais occidentalis Beck, 1836.
Spire high, whorls well-rounded
and with fifteen to twenty-five
curved axial ribs per whorl.
Numerous spiral threads present.
Outer lip greatly flaring, its edge
thickened and the top pointing
upwards. Color ashen-gray.
Common from 33 to 1640 ft (10-
500 m) in depth from Arctic
Canada to off North Carolina.

American Pelican's Foot
2.3 in (6 cm)

Common Pelican's Foot,
Aporrhais pespelecani (Linnaeus,
1758). Spire sharp, the whorls in
the spire with about twelve axial,
elongate knobs. On the last whorl
there is a second row of rounded
knobs. Outer lip expanded above
and below, as well as having two or
three extensions on the greatly
expanded central part. Color
cream–tan. Lives partially buried
in mud offshore. Abundant from
Norway to the Mediterranean.

Common Pelican's Foot
1.2 in (3 cm)

MacAndrew's Pelican's Foot,
Aporrhais serresianus (Michaud,
1828). Shell similar to the
Common Pelican's Foot, but it is
smaller, with thinner, longer, more
delicate spines, and with weaker,
more numerous axial ribs and
knobs. *A. macandreae* Jeffreys,
1867, is a synonym. Deep water
from the northern British Isles to
Norway.

**MacAndrew's Pelican's
Foot**
0.8 in (2 cm)

Trivias
(*Family Eratoidae*)

Known as members of the "allied cowries," these small, bright
shells resemble the true tropical cowries in shape only. Most
live in warm seas, but there are three exceptions in western
Europe where some of them are popularly called "groats" or
"nuns." They have a colorful mantle which extends up over the
shell. There is no operculum. The trivias are shallow-water
dwellers and feed upon compound ascidians.

Nun Trivia, *Trivia monacha* (da Costa, 1778). Shell globular, solid, with about twenty-eight strong, neat cords running over the rounded top surface. Aperture narrow, with about sixteen small teeth on the concave columellar side. Color brownish pink with three diffused, darker spots on the top. Moderately common under stones and within rock crevices at the low tide mark. Ranges from the British Isles to the Mediterranean.

Nun Trivia
0.8 in (2 cm)

Arctic Trivia, *Trivia arctica* (Pulteney, 1799). Shell globular, solid, resembling the Nun Trivia, but smaller, with fewer ribs, pinkish, and lacking the dorsal spots. This species lives in deeper waters as well as intertidally. Its range extends from Norway to the Mediterranean.

Arctic Trivia
0.6 in (1.5 cm)

Flea Trivia, *Trivia pulex* (Link, 1807). Shell small, globular-elongate, pinkish brown, glossy on the top surface and whitish on the apertural side. Ribs very fine and numerous, with about eighteen to twenty on the columella. This is an intertidal warm-water species occurring in the Mediterranean, the Azores and north into Portugal.

Flea Trivia
0.3 in (1 cm)

Cowries and Bonnets

(*Families Cypraeidae and Cassidae*)

The cowrie family is limited to warm waters, but one species from the Mediterranean reaches north into Portugal. The colorful, glossy shell, with its narrow, toothed aperture, is made by the fleshy mantle that extends over the entire shell. There is no operculum.

The bonnets are small representatives of larger, tropical helmet shells of the family Cassidae.

Agate Cowrie, *Cypraea achatidea* Sowerby, 1837. Shell globular-elongate, glossy; upper surface with dense specklings and blotches of rich, dark-brown. Underside of shell and outer lip white. Teeth on either side of the narrow aperture are very small, the outer lip bearing about twenty to twenty-five. Uncommon in 3 to 100 ft (1–30 m). This is a southern species ranging from Portugal to West Africa.

Agate Cowrie
1.2 in (3 cm)

Rugose Bonnet, *Galeodea rugosa* (Linnaeus, 1771). Shell fairly thin but strong. Sculpture of fine spiral threads and with a single row of small round knobs on the shoulder. Aperture glossy-white, the inner wall quite wide, and the outer lip bearing a few, very small teeth. A common variable species of the Mediterranean but extends northward to the southern parts of the British Isles.

Rugose Bonnet
2.5 in (6 cm)

Mediterranean Bonnet, *Phalium granulatum* subspecies *undulatum* (Gmelin, 1791). Whorls bearing deep, thin, spiral grooves and with six or seven spiral rows of squarish, light-brown dots. Common in the Mediterranean and Azores, but rare as far north as Portugal.

Mediterranean Bonnet
3 in (7.5 cm)

◆

Moon Snails
(*Family Naticidae*)

The clam-eating moon snails are worldwide in distribution and are sand-dwellers, usually in shallow water. The operculum completely seals the aperture and may be soft and chitinous, as in *Neverita*, or may be hard and shelly, as in *Natica*. The females lay a circular, sand-covered collar into which the minute eggs are buried. In England they are called necklace-shells.

Drake's Moon Snail, *Neverita draconis* (Dall, 1903). Shell globular, with well-rounded, grayish whorls. Umbilicus quite wide and deep. The upper part of the columella has a very small, swollen callus. The periostracum is absent on the whorls, but often remaining within the umbilicus. A southern offshore species ranging from Baja California to Oregon.

Drake's Moon Snail
2.4 in (6 cm)

Shark Eye, *Neverita duplicata* (Say, 1822). A slightly flattened, globular, glossy, gray shell characterized by a deep umbilicus covered over by a large, button-like, brown callus. Columella white. A common, shallow-water sand-flat species with a large plough-like forefoot and reduced tentacles. Ranges from Massachusetts to Texas.

Shark Eye
2.5 in (6.5 cm)

Josephine's Moon Snail, *Neverita josephinia* (Risso, 1826). Globular, but flattened from above; glossy gray to yellowish brown above and whitish underneath. Aperture chocolate. Umbilicus filled by a brown, flattened callus. A Mediterranean sandflat-dweller, ranging north into Portugal.

Josephine's Moon Snail
1.5 in (4 cm)

Spotted Northern Moon Snail, *Lunatia triseriata* (Say, 1822). A small, drab, globular shell with a small, deep umbilicus. Usually covered by a dull, thin, tan periostracum. Color of shell cream, the last whorl bears three spiral rows of twelve to fourteen bluish or reddish brown square spots. The borders of the sandy egg collar are crimped, rather than smooth as in *L. heros*. Common in shallow water to 100 ft (30 m) depth in coarse sand where it drills holes in small tellin clams. Ranges from eastern Canada to off North Carolina.

Spotted Northern Moon Snail
0.5 in (1.2 cm)

Common Northern Moon Snail, *Lunatia heros* (Say, 1822). Shell large, globular, relatively thin-shelled but strong. Umbilicus deep, round, not very large, and only slightly covered by a thickening of the columella wall. Color dirty-white to brownish gray. Aperture glossy, tan or with purplish brown stains. Periostracum thin, light yellow-brown. Operculum chitinous, thin and light-brown. Egg case, with minute eggs embedded in it, is a wide, circular ribbon of sand, flexible when wet, but crumbles when dry. A common intertidal species ranging from the Gulf of St. Lawrence, Canada, to off North Carolina.

Common Northern Moon Snail
4 in (10 cm)

Lewis' Moon Snail, *Lunatia lewisi* (Gould, 1847). A heavy, globular shell, slightly shouldered a little distance below the suture. Umbilicus deep, round and narrow. Characterized by the brown-stained, rather small, button-like callus partially obscuring the top edge of the umbilicus. A very common clam-eating species found in 3 to 165 ft (1–50 m) of water from British Columbia to southern California.

Lewis' Moon Snail
4 in (10 cm)

European Necklace Shell, *Lunatia catena* (da Costa, 1776). Shell globular, with smooth, well-rounded whorls. Suture distinct. Umbilicus fairly large, deep and rounded. The upper half of the columella is swollen and glossy-white. Color of shell tan with a row of slanting, short, dark-brown streaks just below the suture. Early whorls with a row of tan spots. Operculum chitinous and thin. Sandy egg collars wash ashore in the summer. A common, clam-eating dweller of intertidal sand-flats down to a depth of 410 ft (125 m). Ranges from the British Isles to the Mediterranean.

European Necklace Shell
1.5 in (4 cm)

Alder's Moon Snail, *Lunatia alderi* (Forbes, 1838). Shell small and globular with a short, depressed spire. Exterior glossy smooth. Umbilicus small, deep, partially covered by the brownish, glossy columella. Exterior tan with five spiral rows of chestnut-brown arrow-shaped, short streaks. The animal covers the shell with its foot. The forefoot, used for digging, covers the short tentacles and eyes. Lives from the intertidal sand-flats to deep, offshore waters where it feeds on tellin clams. Ranges from Norway south to the Mediterranean.

Alder's Moon Snail
0.6 in (1.5 cm)

Guillemin's Moon Snail, *Lunatia guillemini* (Payraudeau, 1826). Globular, with a pointed spire; exterior glossy smooth and solid. Umbilicus narrow and deep, bordered by a wide white band. Columella glossy, narrow, tinged with reddish brown. Aperture dark-brown. Color bluish gray with numerous, dark-brown, intertwining streaks and lines. A common Mediterranean species extending north to the Brittany coast of France.

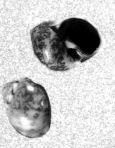

Guillemin's Moon Snail
1 in (2.5 cm)

Pale Northern Moon Snail, *Lunatia pallida* (Broderip and Sowerby, 1829). Globular, smooth, pure-white and covered with a thin, yellowish periostracum. Inner wall of aperture moderately thickened with a white glaze. Umbilicus almost closed. Operculum chitinous and translucent brown. A common, widely dispersed Arctic species found south to California and south to off North

Pale Northern Moon Snail
1.5 in (4 cm)

Carolina. Present in Scandinavia and rare in the North Sea. Lives on clay and sandy-mud bottoms from 32 to 6560 ft (10–2000 m).

Dusky Moon Snail, *Lunatia fusca* (Blainville, 1825). Shell small, globular with a low rounded spire. Color brown to chestnut but, when fresh, covered with a dull, dark periostracum. Columella glossy, dark-brown with the base and lower aperture white. The columella is swollen where a spiral, rounded ridge emerges from the deep umbilicus. The soft parts are reddish brown. This is a southern Mediterranean species which extends northward into the British Isles wherever there is shallow water and a muddy sand bottom.

Dusky Moon Snail
1.2 in (3 cm)

Smith's Moon Snail, *Bulbus smithi* (Brown, 1839). Shell lightweight, globular, rather fragile, and with a bright straw-colored or golden periostracum covering the shell, whose surface is minutely reticulated by spiral threads and growth lines. Aperture very large. Middle of columella is indented on the left. Uncommon offshore from Labrador to the Georges Banks of Massachusetts.

Smith's Moon Snail
1 in (2.5 cm)

Iceland Moon Snail, *Amauropsis islandicus* (Gmelin, 1791). Shell globular, somewhat lightweight, with a strongly channeled suture. The rounded, smooth whorls are covered with a thin, yellowish brown periostracum which flakes off when dry. Umbilicus absent or only a slight slit. Columella narrow and glossy white. Operculum with few whorls, chitinous and

Iceland Moon Snail
1.3 in (3 cm)

translucent brown and with microscopic spiral lines. A moderately common, cold-water moon snail found just offshore down to 525 ft (160 m). It is a circumpolar species extending south to off Virginia and to the North Sea and Scandinavia.

Purplish Moon Snail,
Amauropsis purpurea Dall, 1871. Very similar to the Iceland Moon Snail but smaller and with a purplish-green periostracum and shallower sutural channels. Possibly only a subspecies which ranges from Alaska to British Columbia, Canada. Members of this genus lay a sandy egg collar in which are set single, large eggs which hatch into miniature, crawling snails. They feed on bivalves.

Purplish Moon Snail
0.7 in (2 cm)

Oldroyd's Fragile Moon Snail,
Calinaticina oldroydii (Dall, 1897). Shell globular, rather thin-shelled, a little wider than high. Umbilicus wide and deep, with the upper part obscured by the expanded upper part of the white, glossy columella. Spiral lines on the outer shell are prominent. The species lives in large colonies in sandy areas offshore where they feed on small bivalves and lay sandy egg collars. Ranges from Oregon to southern California.

Oldroyd's Fragile Moon Snail
2.5 in (6 cm)

Arctic Natica, *Natica clausa* Broderip and Sowerby, 1829. Shell strong, fairly thin-shelled, smooth, yellowish white, with a smooth gray to yellowish brown periostracum. Whorls evenly well-rounded. Umbilicus sealed over by a small, glossy-white, flat callus. Operculum shelly, thin, slightly concave, smooth, white and with only a few whorls. Animal is translucent whitish cream with a large forefoot. A common circumpolar species extending southward through eastern Canada to off North Carolina; south to northern California; and from Scandinavia to off Portugal in deep water.

Arctic Natica
1 in (2.5 cm)

Dillwyn's Natica, *Naticarius dillwyni* (Payraudeau, 1826). Shell small, depressed globular, solid, glossy tan with white bands bearing obscure, arrowhead, chestnut-brown markings. Periostracum thin and yellowish brown. Umbilicus deep, narrow and partially covered by the glossy end of an umbilical cord. Operculum shelly, ivory-colored, paucispiral and bordered by a deep groove and a raised spiral cord. Found on sand from 15 to 30 ft (4–10 m), from Portugal south into the Mediterranean.

Dillwyn's Natica
0.7 in (2 cm)

Fly-specked Natica, *Naticarius stercusmuscarum*, (Gmelin, 1791). Thin- but strong-shelled, smooth, globular, cream-colored with numerous, irregularly placed, small dots of light-brown. Umbilicus fairly large and deep with a large, rounded spiral cord emerging from within and ending at the middle part of the narrow, glossy columella. Operculum shelly, dirty-white, with a dozen, distinct, sharp, crowded spiral ridges. Appears in Italian fish markets. A common shallow-water, Mediterranean species extending north into Portuguese waters.

Fly-specked Natica
2 in (5 cm)

Tritons and Dove-shells
(*Families Ranellidae and Columbellidae*)

Most members of the triton family, Ranellidae (formerly Cymatiidae), are warm-water dwellers, but one, the Oregon Triton, has ventured into the cold waters of northwest America. Cold-water forms have a thick, hairy periostracum. The numerous, small-shelled dove-shells are found worldwide, usually occurring as large colonies in shallow water. The operculum is chitinous and sickle-shaped. The foot narrow and the siphonal canal long. They are aggressive carnivores.

Oregon Triton, *Fusitriton oregonensis* (Redfield, 1848). Shell fusiform, with about six whorls, all convex in outline and bearing sixteen to eighteen axial riblets nodulated by the crossing of smaller spiral pairs of threads. The periostracum is heavy, spiculose, bristle-like and gray-brown. Common near shore from Alaska to British Columbia; in deeper water south to San Diego.

Oregon Triton
3 in (7.5 cm)

Variegated Dove-shell, *Astyris tuberosa* (Carpenter, 1865). Shell very small, slender, with a narrow, pointed, flat-sided spire; exterior smooth, usually glossy, tan with light-brown flames and spots. Outer lip thickened and with small teeth within. Common from 6 to 195 ft (2–60 m) from Alaska to California.

Variegated Dove-shell
0.4 in (8 mm)

Rosy Northern Dove-shell, *Astyris rosacea* (Gould, 1841). Very small, slender, dingy-white to rose, with a reddish apex. Smooth, except for microscopic spiral lines. A common circumboreal species found offshore in Alaska, Greenland to off New Jersey; and Norway to Portugal.

Rosy Northern Dove-shell
0.4 in (8 mm)

Lunar Dove-shell, *Astyris lunata* (Say, 1826). Shell very small, glossy, smooth, translucent gray and marked with fine, axial zigzag brown to yellow stripes. Base of shell with fine incised lines. Aperture constricted and slightly sinuate. Outer lip with four small teeth on the inside. No prominent varix. Nuclear whorls very small and translucent. A very common, shallow-water species associated with weedy areas. Ranges from southern Massachusetts to Texas and to Brazil.

Lunar Dove-shell
0.2 in (5 mm)

Joseph's Coat Amphissa, *Amphissa versicolor* Dall, 1871. Shell elongate to ovate, rather thin-shelled but strong; with seven glossy whorls which bear about fifteen obliquely slanting, strong, rounded axial ribs. Numerous spiral, incised lines are strongest on the base of the body whorl. Lower columella area has a small shield. Outer lip thickened within by about a dozen small, white teeth. Color pinkish gray with indistinct mottlings of orange-brown. This is a common intertidal species found as deep as 65 ft (20 m). Occurs from British Columbia to off Baja California.

Joseph's Coat Amphissa
0.5 in (1.2 cm)

Columbian Amphissa, *Amphissa columbiana* Dall, 1916. Similar to Joseph's Coat Amphissa but twice as large and with twenty to twenty-four weaker, vertical, axial riblets on the last whorl. There is a low, rounded varix behind the outer lip. Color yellow-brown with indistinct mauve mottlings. Periostracum thin and yellowish. Operculum chitinous and brown. Moderately common in shallow water from Alaska to Oregon; rarely off the southern Californian coast.

Columbian Amphissa
1 in (2.5 cm)

Murex and Rock Shells
(*Family Muricidae*)

This is a very diverse and widely distributed family of carnivorous snails. The sexes are separate, and they have a strong set of radular teeth and a tough, horny operculum. Eggs are laid in clusters or balls of leathery capsules.

Purple Dye Murex, *Bolinus brandaris* (Linnaeus, 1758). Shell with a swollen body whorl, ovate aperture and a long, straight siphonal canal. Sculpture of two rows of about six or seven strong, short, straight spines on each whorl. The species is mainly Mediterranean, but is found as far north as Portugal.

Purple Dye Murex
2.5 in (6 cm)

Trunculus Murex, *Hexaplex trunculus* (Linnaeus, 1758). Shell broadly fusiform, with a short, broad siphonal canal twisted to the left. Axial ribs and former lips have an open spine at the shoulder. Color brownish with two or three narrow, spiral bands of white. It is common in the Mediterranean, and rare as far north as Portugal.

Trunculus Murex
2 in (5 cm)

Foliated Thorn Purpura, *Ceratostoma foliatum* (Gmelin, 1791). Solid, heavy shell with three large, thin, foliaceous varices per whorl which are finely fimbriated on the anterior side. Numerous small spiral cords present. Siphonal canal closed along its length, its tip turned up. Base of outer lip with a small, strong spine. Exterior white to light-brown. Found on rocks near shore, where it feeds on mussels and barnacles, commonly from southern Alaska to northern California.

Foliated Thorn Drupa
2.5 in (6 cm)

Atlantic Oyster Drill, *Urosalpinx cinerea* (Say 1822). Broadly fusiform, without axial varices but having about nine to eleven rounded, axial ribs per whorl and with numerous, strong spiral cords. Outer lip slightly thickened on the inside and sometimes with two to six small, whitish teeth. Color a dirty-gray or yellowish with irregular, brown spiral bands. Aperture brown. This common, shallow-water species is very destructive to oysters. Ranges from Nova Scotia to northeast Florida. Introduced prior to 1888 to Washington and central California. Later introduced to England.

Atlantic Oyster Drill
0.8 in (2 cm)

Lurid Dwarf Triton, *Urosalpinx lurida* (Middendorff, 1848). Fusiform, with rounded whorls, elongate spire, and numerous, rough, rounded spiral cords crossing eight to ten weak, rounded axial ribs. Six to eight small teeth are on the inside of the outer lip. Color variable, whitish to rusty-brown, sometimes banded. Periostracum dark-brown and fuzzy. Siphonal canal usually sealed along its length. Very common in rocky intertidal areas from southern Alaska to northern California; rarer to the south.

Lurid Dwarf Triton
1 in (2.5 cm)

Spindle Dwarf Triton, *Urosalpinx fusulus* (Brocchi, 1814). Shell fusiform; six whorls, slightly shouldered, with nine or ten rounded, axial ribs crossed by numerous, spiral cords which form two rows of low tubercles in the whorls in the spire. Siphonal canal fairly long, open along its length. Columella glossy white. Inside of outer lip with four or five strong, short teeth. Suture well-indented. Spire pointed; nuclear whorls brown and glassy. Aperture darker within. Operculum chitinous, heavy and brown. Moderately common in rocky shallow areas in the Mediterranean and western Europe.

Spindle Dwarf Triton
0.8 in (2 cm)

Edwards' Dwarf Winkle, *Ocinebrina edwardsii* (Payraudeau, 1826). Shell small, broadly fusiform, six whorls, slightly shouldered. Sculpture of about sixteen elongate, rounded axial ribs per whorl crossed by numerous, fine, irregular threads, usually a lighter tan. Columella smooth, stained glossy tan. Inside swollen outer lip are six or seven short teeth. Siphonal canal short, closed off on apertural side. Interior of aperture purplish tan. A shallow-water, hard-bottom species common in the Mediterranean and northward into Portugal.

Edwards' Dwarf Winkle
0.8 in (2 cm)

Sharp Dwarf Winkle, *Ocinebrina aciculata* (Lamarck, 1822). Shell small, broadly fusiform, heavily ornamented with eight to ten slanting, rounded, axial ribs crossed by delicately fimbriated, spiral threads. Siphonal canal short, usually closed along its length. Six or seven elongated teeth are within the outer lip. Spire pointed. Color tan to orange-buff. Umbilicus chink-like. Soft parts red with flecks of yellow. They probably feed upon small, intertidal barnacles. Common from southern British Isles to the Mediterranean.

Sharp Dwarf Winkle
0.7 in (2 cm)

Spotted Thorn Drupe, *Acanthina spirata* (Blainville, 1832). Low-spired, solid, smoothish, except for numerous, poorly developed, spiral threads. Spine on lower outer lip is strong, behind which on the base of the outside of the body whorl is a weak spiral groove. Whorls slightly shouldered. Color bluish gray with numerous rows of small, red-brown dots. Aperture within is bluish white. Rarely, all-yellow forms occurs. Common at high-tide mark along rocky shores and among beds of mussels upon which they feed. Ranges from Puget Sound, Washington, to southern California.

Spotted Thorn Drupe
1.2 in (3 cm)

Crested Dwarf Triton,
Muricopsis cristatus (Brocchi,
1814). Shell slender and fusiform
with a pointed spire and slightly
shouldered whorls. Low axial
rounded ribs are made knobby
because of spiral cords. Color
brown with two broad spiral bands
of yellowish. Columella pinkish,
glossy and with two indistinct
beads near the bottom. Outer lip
thick and recurved, and with three
coarse white teeth. Siphonal canal
fairly long and open along its
length. Intertidal rocky areas in the
Mediterranean to Senegal and to
southern Portugal.

Crested Dwarf Triton
1 in (2.5 cm)

Thick-lipped Drill, *Eupleura
caudata* (Say, 1822). Shell fusiform
and dorso-ventrally compressed
and with two lateral varices. Apex
pointed; siphonal canal moderately
long, almost closed, coming to a
sharp point below. Last varix large,
rounded and with small nodules.
Inside of outer lip with about six
small, bead-like teeth. Whorls with
small spiral cords and strong axial
ribs. There are four to six axial ribs
between the last two varices. An
abundant shallow-water species
that feeds by boring into young
oysters. Ranges from south of
Cape Cod to northern Florida.

Thick-lipped Drill
1 in (2.5 cm)

Frilled Dogwinkle, *Nucella
lamellosa* (Gmelin, 1791). Solid,
with a fairly high spire. Columella
almost vertical and straight, not
flattened. Sculpturing and color
very variable: white, grayish, cream
or orange, sometimes spirally
banded. Smoothish or with
foliated ribs. Sometimes spinose. A
very common rock-loving species

Frilled Dogwinkle
2 in (5 cm)

extending from the Bering Straits, Alaska, to central California.

Atlantic Dogwinkle, *Nucella lapillus* (Linnaeus, 1758). Broadly fusiform; spire usually elevated. Exterior either smoothish or sculptured with rounded, spiral ridges which may be finely fimbriated. Color usually dull-white, but in many specimens yellowish, orange or brownish. Rarely with dark-brown spiral bands. In some areas of New England there are colonies of strongly fimbriated specimens. This abundant species lives on rocky coasts between tide marks where it feeds upon barnacles and small mussels. The animal gives off a tyrian purple dye once used as an indelible laundry marking ink. The species ranges from southern Labrador to New York; from Norway to northern Portugal.

Atlantic Dogwinkle
1.5 in (4 cm)

Emarginate Dogwinkle, *Nucella emarginata* (Deshayes, 1839). With a rather short spire. Aperture large. Columella strongly arched, flattened and slightly concave below. Sculpturing variable, but characteristically with coarse spiral cords, usually alternatingly small and large. Cords often scaled or coarsely noduled. Exterior dirty-gray to rusty-brown, sometimes with darker spiral bands. Aperture and columella light-brown. A very common rock-dwelling, coastal species ranging from Alaska to southern California.

Emarginate Dogwinkle
1 in (2.5 cm)

File Dogwinkle, *Nucella lima* (Gmelin, 1791). Broadly fusiform, with a low spire, rounded whorls with seventeen to twenty round-topped, smooth, crowded spiral cords, the latter often alternating in size. Color whitish or orange-brown, rarely banded. This is a common, cold-water, intertidal species ranging from northern Japan and Alaska to northern California.

File Dogwinkle
1.2 in (3 cm)

Channeled Dogwinkle, *Nucella canaliculata* (Duclos, 1832). Shell solid, elongate-globose, with about fourteen to sixteen low, flat-topped, closely spaced spiral cords on the body whorl. Suture slightly channeled. Color white or orange-brown, often spirally banded. This is a moderately common intertidal species feeding on mussels and barnacles in rocky areas. Ranges from the Aleutian Islands to central California.

Channeled Dogwinkle
1 in (2.5 cm)

Sting Winkle, *Ocenebra erinacea* (Linnaeus, 1758). Shell broadly fusiform with an angulate, acute spire. Whorls shouldered and sculptured by seven or eight thin, erect, evenly spaced axial ribs, crossed by numerous, rounded, finely fimbriated cords. Siphonal canal closed along its length and fairly long, with a scarred siphonal fasciole alongside. Aperture oval. Outer lip often bounded by a thin, well-developed varix. Exterior yellowish, often with brown bandings. Common below low tide mark in rocky areas where they feed on bivalves. In the spring they lay clusters of urn-shaped egg capsules. Ranges from southern British Isles to the Azores and the Mediterranean.

Sting Winkle
1.5 in (4 cm)

Poulson's Dwarf Triton,
Ocenebra poulsoni (Carpenter,
1864). Shell solid, with a semi-
gloss finish. Whorls with eight or
nine nodulated, rounded, axial ribs
per whorl crossed by numerous,
very fine, incised spiral lines on the
ribs. Siphonal canal narrowly
open. Periostracum thin, grayish
or brownish and smooth. Aperture
white. A very common species on
rocks and wharf pilings, especially
in the southern part of its range,
from California to Mexico.

Poulson's Dwarf Triton
1.5 in (4 cm)

Clathrate Trophon, *Boreotrophon
clathratus* (Linnaeus, 1758). Shell
fusiform, dull-white, with a deep
suture which may have a flat area
just below it. Siphonal canal well-
developed and open along its side.
Whorls with strong, thin axial ribs
which are hollow in front. In many
specimens the tops of the ribs are
rounded, but in others they may be
protruding up into small
projections. Aperture white, and
outer lip slightly flaring. Young
specimens have a fairly long
siphonal canal. A moderately
common dweller of mud bottoms
offshore in Arctic Seas. It extends
into the waters of Maine and
Norway.

Clathrate Trophon
1.5 in (4 cm)

Northwest Pacific Trophon,
Boreotrophon pacificus (Dall, 1902).
Shell white, fusiform, similar to the
Clathrate Trophon, but the length
of the aperture and siphonal canal
is more than half the length of the
entire shell. The well-rounded
whorls have twelve to twenty ribs
which are slightly shouldered just
below the well-indented suture.
This carnivorous species is fairly

Northwest Pacific Trophon
1 in (2.5 cm)

common at the low tide area in
Alaska, but further south it is
found offshore in deep water. It
also occurs in Canadian Arctic
waters.

Stuart's Trophon, *Boreotrophon
stuarti* (E. A. Smith, 1880).
Broadly fusiform, pure-white to
yellow-cream and with a waxy
texture. Each of the five or six
whorls has nine to eleven strong,
thin, lamella-like, high-shouldered
ribs. Whorls in the spire are
cancellated by two or three spiral
raised threads. Body whorl with
five very weak spiral, rounded
threads. Uncommon from low tide
down to about 165 ft (50 m).
Extends from Alaska to off San
Diego, California.

Stuart's Trophon
2 in (5 cm)

Alaskan Trophon, *Boreotrophon
alaskanus* (Dall, 1902). Shell
cream-white, fusiform, with the
whorls almost detached. The
suture is very deep and there is a
flat, spiral gutter adjacent to it.
There are about nine varices per
whorl with the tops extending
upwards in the form of open flutes.
Siphonal canal fairly long. This
attractive species ranges from
northern Japan to the Bering Sea
in deep water.

Alaskan Trophon
1.3 in (3 cm)

Truncate Trophon, *Boreotrophon
truncatus* (Strom, 1768). Shell
white, fusiform with a sharp
conical spire. Suture deep and
bounded below by a slightly
flattened, narrow gutter. Fifteen to
twenty-five ribs on the last whorl,
strongest at the top and fading out
towards the base of the shell.
Color yellowish brown. Columella

and aperture glossy-white. Outer lip thin and smooth. No umbilicus. A common, cold-water, circumpolar species occurring in offshore waters south to the Georges Banks, Massachusetts; Alaska; Greenland south to the Bay of Biscay, France.

Truncate Trophon
0.6 in (1.5 cm)

Latticed Trophon, *Boreotrophon craticulatus* (Fabricius, 1780). Shell fusiform, of a creamy waxy consistency with the top of the whorls shouldered and bearing about ten delicate, thin, semi-translucent, axial varices. There are numerous very small spiral cords that cross the riblets and give the shell a slightly latticed appearance. Aperture half the length of the entire shell and narrowing below into a fairly short, open siphonal canal. Nuclear whorls distinct, bulbous and glassy smooth. *B. fabricii* (Moller, 1842) is a synonym. It lives in about 196 ft (60 m) of water from Arctic Canada to Nova Scotia.

Latticed Trophon
1 in (2.5 cm)

Buccinum Whelks
(*Family Buccinidae*)

This is a family of large, cold-water univalves, known in England as buckies and whelks. They are offshore-dwellers, many of which are found in fish markets and also serve as food for bottom-feeding fish. All have a chitinous, brown operculum.

Common Northern Buccinum
or **Buckie**, *Buccinum undatum*
Linnaeus, 1758, is the best known
of the northern edible whelks.
Shell solid, chalky-gray to
yellowish brown, with a
moderately thick, gray
periostracum. Axial ribs slanting,
nine to eighteen per whorl, low,
rounded and extending quarter to
half the way down the whorl.
Common in shallow water in the
lower Arctic Seas as far south as
New Jersey and the British Isles.

**Common Northern
Buccinum**
3 in (7.5 cm)

Totten's Buccinum, *Buccinum
totteni* Stimpson, 1865. Thin-
shelled, with five or six large, well-
rounded, smoothish whorls.
Aperture slightly less than half the
length of the shell. Color yellow-
brown with a thin, straw-colored
periostracum. Spiral sculpture of
numerous, finely incised striations.
Ranges from Arctic Canada to
Maine; Greenland and Iceland.

Totten's Buccinum
2 in (5 cm)

Plectrum Buccinum, *Buccinum
plectrum* Stimpson, 1865. Shell
thin-shelled but strong. Aperture
about one third the length of the
shell. Numerous axial, rounded
ribs slanting and limited to the
upper third of the whorl. Spiral
sculpture of numerous, crowded,
rough threads. Color grayish to
yellowish white. Common offshore
in Arctic waters south to Puget
Sound; and south to the Gulf of
St. Lawrence, Canada.

Plectrum Buccinum
2.5 in (6 cm)

Glacial Buccinum, *Buccinum
glaciale* Linnaeus, 1761. A fairly
thick, sturdy shell, but lightweight
in comparison to its size.
Characterized by its thick, glossy,

white, flaring, reflected outer lip,
and by the two wavy, strong spiral
cords on the periphery of the
whorls. Spiral incised lines
numerous. Suture narrow and
deep. Color mauve-brown.
Aperture cream with a purplish
flush within. Common from low
tide to several feet. Ranges in the
Arctic Seas to Washington State
and south to the Gulf of St.
Lawrence.

Glacial Buccinum
2.5 in (6 cm)

Angulate Buccinum, *Buccinum
angulosum* Gray, 1839. Shell solid,
similar to the Glacial Buccinum,
but with a shorter spire. Aperture
half the length of the entire shell.
Early whorls smooth. Post-nuclear
whorls with numerous, rounded
axial ribs extending from suture to
suture. Later whorls with fewer,
widely spaced, short, slanting ribs
which are sometimes stained rusty-
brown. Between the ribs the shell
is slightly concave and may bear
one or two weak spiral threads.
Columella enamel-white, slightly
twisted below. Outer lip flaring,
thickened and smooth. Occurs in
the European and Canadian Arctic
waters as well as the Bering Straits.

Angulate Buccinum
2.5 in (6 cm)

Finmark Buccinum, *Buccinum
finmarkianum* Verkrüzen, 1875.
Shell oblong-ovate, thin-shelled,
smooth, yellowish white with a
thin, yellowish periostracum.
Whorls well-rounded. Sculpture
sometimes with very faint spiral
threads. Suture neatly indented.
Columella and aperture enamel-
white. Outer lip thin, smooth and
slightly flaring below. Operculum
small, almost circular, chitinous
and translucent yellow. An

Finmark Buccinum
2.5 in (6 cm)

uncommon species found off
Norway.

Silky Buccinum, *Buccinum
scalariforme* Moller, 1842. Aperture
half the length of the entire shell.
Whorls in spire and the upper two-
thirds of the last whorl with
numerous, strong, narrow,
slanting, axial ribs which are
sometimes intertwining. Outer lip
slightly sinuate, thin and slightly
flaring. Spiral sculpture of microscopic, beaded threads giving the
surface a silky appearance. Color
light-brown but covered with a
dark, thin periostracum. *B. tenue*
Gray is a synonym. Common
offshore down to 655 ft (200 m).
Arctic Seas to Washington State;
and south to the Gulf of Maine.

Silky Buccinum
2 in (5 cm)

Polar Buccinum, *Buccinum
polare* Gray, 1839. Similar to the
Silky Buccinum, but the shell is
more globose, with a lower spire
and broader, more flaring, sharper,
smooth outer lip. Axial riblets
more numerous, much smaller,
and crossed by numerous spiral
threads which form distinct beads
and a latticed effect. Columella
and aperture glossy yellowish
white. Periostracum thin, light-
brown. A cold-water circumpolar
species extending southward to
northern Japan, Alaska and to
Greenland.

Polar Buccinum
2.5 in (6 cm)

Flaky Buccinum, *Buccinum
hydrophanum* Hancock, 1846.
Shell with a tall spire, an aperture
about one third the length of the
entire shell. Whorls rounded,
smoothish. Siphonal fasciole
absent. Fine growth lines may be

present. Outer lip thin, sharp and flaring somewhat below. Color pale yellowish brown. This carnivorous species lives from 330 to 3935 ft (100–1200 m) on muddy bottoms. It is an Arctic species ranging across Canada to the Grand Banks and in Europe south to the Shetland Islands.

Flaky Buccinum
3 in (7.5 cm)

Humphrey's Buccinum, *Buccinum humphreysianum* Bennett, 1824. Thin-shelled, broadly oval with smoothish, well-rounded whorls. Spire regularly conic, the aperture about half the length of the entire shell. Siphonal canal short and wide. Outer lip thin and fragile. Surface with extremely fine spiral threads crossed by fine, slanting growth lines. Periostracum very thin, yellowish with occasional weak brownish streaks. An uncommon, deep-water species found in Arctic Seas in Japan, Canada and northwestern Europe as far south as off Portugal.

Humphrey's Buccinum
3 in (7.5 cm)

Baer's Buccinum, *Buccinum baeri* (Middendorff, 1848). Shell small, ovate-elongate, smoothish, with a beachworn appearance. Aperture a little more than half the length of the shell. Spiral sculpture of very weak, smooth, narrow threads. Growth lines crude on the last whorl. Exterior color light-brown. Range is from the Aleutians to Kodiak Island, Alaska.

Baer's Buccinum
1.5 in (4 cm)

Finely-striate Buccinum, *Buccinum striatissimum* Sowerby, 1899. Shell fairly large, relatively thin-shelled, whitish, with a high acute spire and an aperture one third the length of the shell. Whorls very well-rounded, the suture well-indented. Surface covered with very fine spiral threads. Growth lines weak, but made more evident when the thin, gray periostracum is worn away. Siphonal notch short, narrow but distinct. Interior of aperture white. Occurs in deep water from Japan to Alaska; uncommon.

Finely-striate Buccinum
3.5 in (9 cm)

Norwegian Volute Whelk, *Volutopsius norvegicus* (Gmelin, 1791). Shell large, copious, with a tall spire and a large aperture about half the length of the shell. Whorls well-rounded, smoothish, except for very fine growth lines. Suture finely indented and sometimes with small wrinkles below it. Outer lip smooth, enamel-white and reflected in the upper half. The lower edge is confluent with the hardly evident siphonal region. It is moderately common in cold water south to the Gulf of St. Lawrence; Newfoundland; Scotland and Scandinavia.

Norwegian Volute Whelk
5 in (12.5 cm)

Melon Volute Whelk, *Volutopsius melonis* (Dall, 1891). Shell large, spire short, aperture two-thirds the length of the shell. Two nuclear whorls, smooth, white. Remainder of whorls have crowded, well-rounded, straight, axial ribs crossed by very numerous, crowded, rounded, rough spiral threads. Color ashen purplish gray with a white, narrow columella. An uncommon deep-water species from northern Japan and the Bering Sea.

Melon Volute Whelk
5 in (12.5 cm)

Chestnut Buccinum, *Volutopsius castaneus* (Mörch, 1858). Shell fusiform, rather solid, with four whorls, the early one being bulbous and smooth. Aperture large, slightly larger than half the length of the shell and slightly flaring above. Siphonal canal weakly defined. Exterior surface brownish and smoothish, except for coarse axial wrinkles appearing more as deformities. Moderately common on rocks offshore from the Aleutians to Kodiak Islands, Alaska.

Chestnut Volute Whelk
3 in (7.5 cm)

Sinistral Arctic Whelk, *Pyrolofusus deformis* (Reeve, 1847) is one of the few normally "left-handed" or sinistrally coiling whelks in the northern hemisphere. Shell solid, sinistral, whitish gray, with many low, irregular spiral cords. Nuclear whorls bulbous. Aperture with a thin slightly waved outer lip and enamel-white with brown staining within. Uncommon offshore in the Arctic Seas; Alaska, Greenland and northwestern Europe.

Sinistral Arctic Whelk
3 in (7.5 cm)

Behring's Neptune, *Beringion behringi* (Middendorff, 1844). Shell large, fusiform, dextral, with four or five well-rounded whorls, the first two smooth and bulbous, but usually badly eroded. Suture coarsely indented. Aperture slightly more than half the length of entire shell. Siphonal canal well-developed but short. Outer lip not flaring, but thin, smooth and strong. Exterior has five or six weak spiral cords and weak, coarse, low ribs. There is an eroded look to this purplish brown

Behring's Neptune
3 in (7.5 cm)

shell. Formerly called *Beringius beringi*. Uncommon offshore in the Bering Sea.

Kennicott's Neptune, *Beringion kennicottii* (Dall, 1907). Shell large, not very heavy. Characterized by about nine strong, arched, somewhat rounded axial ribs extending from suture to suture and, on the body whorl, extending three-quarters the way down. Spiral sculpture of microscopic scratches, except on the base where there are a dozen or so weak threads. Periostracum light-brown, thin and usually flakes off from dried specimens. Shell chalky-gray. Moderately common offshore from 9 to 165 ft (3–50 m) from the Aleutians to Cook's Inlet, Alaska.

Kennicott's Neptune
3.5 in (9 cm)

Turton's Neptune, *Neoberingius turtoni* (Bean, 1834). Shell large, broadly fusiform, thin-shelled but strong; two nuclear whorls bulbous, white and smooth. Spire acute, tall, with well-rounded whorls bearing numerous, weakly beaded spiral threads. Aperture less than half the length of the entire shell. Outer lip thin, sharp but strong. Siphonal canal produced below and open. Color whitish gray. *B. ossiani* (Friele, 1879) is a synonym. Moderately common offshore in the Arctic Seas, Scandinavia south to the North Sea; Labrador to Newfoundland and the Gulf of St. Lawrence.

Turton's Neptune
5 in (12.5 cm)

Pygmy Colus, *Colus pygmaeus* (Gould, 1841). Shell small, fusiform, fairly fragile, with a straight-sided, pointed apex and with rounded whorls. Exterior chalk-white, with numerous fine spiral threads covered with a light olive-gray, thin, smoothish periostracum. Aperture about half the length of the shell. This is one of several boreal species of *Colus* found in the northern hemisphere. This small one extends offshore from the Gulf of St. Lawrence to off North Carolina.

Pygmy Colus
0.8 in (2 cm)

Hairy Colus, *Colus pubescens* (Verrill, 1882). Shell of moderate size, fusiform, solid, with a straight-sided spire. It is similar to the Pygmy Colus, but larger, with a longer aperture and the sutures are not as deeply impressed nor as wide. Spiral sculpture of numerous, crowded incised lines. Periostracum dark-brown, thin, velvety when wet but flakes off when dry. Very commonly dredged from 100 to 3940 ft (30–1200 m) from Arctic Canada to off South Carolina.

Hairy Colus
2.5 in (6 cm)

Simple Colus, *Colus gracilis* (da Costa, 1778). Shell fusiform, elongate, with a tall, straight-sided spire. Protoconch smooth, slightly swollen. Whorls moderately convex and with about sixty low, spiral threads, crossed occasionally by axial growth lines. Aperture oval, cream-white. Columella enamel-white, arched. Siphonal canal fairly long and twisted slightly to the left. Color of shell white, with a yellowish brown, soft periostracum. *C. glaber* (Kobelt) is a synonym. Lives on sandy mud bottoms from 100 to 1970 ft (30–600 m) deep from Norway to off Portugal.

Simple Colus
2.7 in (7 cm)

Spitzbergen Colus, *Colus spitzbergeni* (Reeve, 1855). Spindle-shaped, rather light-shelled. Spire elongate. Whorls well-rounded with twelve to fourteen small, low, flat-topped, equally sized, spiral cords. Periostracum thin, reddish brown. Common offshore from 6 to 852 ft (2–260 m). Arctic Seas to Maine and Scandinavia; Bering Sea to Washington State.

Spitzbergen Colus
3 in (7.5 cm)

Jeffrey's Colus, *Colus jeffreysianus* (Fischer, 1868). Shell fusiform, similar to the Simple Colus, but fatter and with a proportionately longer aperture. The siphonal canal is shorter. Spiral sculpture coarser, with about thirty spiral threads on the last whorl. Shell white, rarely with a pinkish brown tint. Periostracum pale-yellow. A synonym appears to be *turgidulus* (Friele). This carnivorous snail lives on sandy mud bottoms from 195 to 2295 ft (60–700 m). Ranges from Norway to off Spain.

Jeffrey's Colus
2 in (5 cm)

Iceland Colus, *Colus islandicus* (Gmelin, 1791). Shell broadly fusiform. Three nuclear whorls, bulbous, and set obliquely to the rest of the shell. Whorls slightly convex. Siphonal canal long and almost straight. Outer lip thin and strong. Surface whitish, with numerous, fine, subdued, spiral ridges and covered by a pale brownish, smooth periostracum. Aperture about half the length of the shell. Outer lip thin, smooth and strong. These carnivorous snails live on sandy mud bottoms from 32 to 9840 ft (10–3000 m) deep. They lay a leathery, dome-

Iceland Colus
5 in (12.5 cm)

shaped capsule on rocks and each may contain several thousand minute eggs. Ranges in the Arctic Seas from Canada to Scandinavia.

Stimpson's Colus, *Colus stimpsoni* (Mörch, 1867). Fusiform, very similar to the Iceland Colus, but is fatter and has a less produced nuclear whorl. Shell chalky-white, but covered with a semi-glossy, light- to dark-brown, moderately thin periostracum. Sculpture of numerous incised spiral lines. Fairly common from 9 to 3280 ft (3–1000 m). Found off Labrador and Newfoundland south to off North Carolina.

Stimpson's Colus
4 in (10 cm)

Herendeen's Colus, *Colus herendeenii* (Dall, 1902). Shell elongate-fusiform with about seven whorls that are slightly convex. Aperture ovate and less than half the length of the entire shell. Sutures narrow and very deep. Whorls with numerous, deep incised lines, between which are formed flat-topped, narrow spiral cords. Siphonal canal moderately long. Color white and overlaid by a thin, yellowish periostracum. Uncommon off the Aleutian Islands and eastward to the Shumagin Islands, Alaska, in fairly deep water.

Herendeen's Colus
2.7 in (7 cm)

Fat Colus, *Colus ventricosus* (Gmelin, 1791). Shell fusiform but very fat, with well-rounded whorls and an aperture that is slightly longer than half the entire shell. Spiral sculpture of very faint, raised lines. Siphonal canal open along its length and slightly twisted. Outer lip thin, sharp and strong. Color of shell whitish gray. Periostracum velvety, brownish and fairly thick. Uncommon offshore from Nova Scotia to the Georges Banks, Massachusetts.

Ovum Arctic Whelk, *Liomesus ovum* (Turton, 1825). Shell fairly small, ovate-fusiform, smooth, creamy white, and with convex whorls. Nuclear whorls very small. Growth lines not apparent unless the outer lip had been previously broken. Columella short, and with an abrupt twist at the end. Outer lip slightly flaring and round at the base. Parietal wall with a large, glazed white area. Periostracum very thin and translucent. Small round leathery capsules are fastened in a clump to the underside of the female's shell. One of many eggs develops into a single large, crawling young snail. Synonym: *L. dalei* (Sowerby, 1825). It is common in the northern waters of northwestern Europe.

Common Northwest Neptune, *Neptunea lyrata* (Gmelin, 1791). Shell large, broadly fusiform, solid, fairly heavy. With five or six strongly convex whorls bearing about eight strongly to poorly developed, raised spiral cords, two of which usually are seen in each whorl in the spire. Faint spiral threads are also present. Exterior dull whitish brown. Fairly common in Alaska from shore to 330 ft (100 m); off Oregon and northern California it occurs in deeper water.

Fat Colus
2 in (5 cm)

Ovum Arctic Whelk
1.5 in (4 cm)

Common Northwest Neptune
5 in (12.5 cm)

Disreputable Neptune, *Neptunea despecta* (Linnaeus, 1758). Fusiform, usually appearing worn and unattractive. Color dingy-white or brownish tan. Eight whorls very convex, the last being ventricose. Sometimes spirally banded with light chestnut. Spiral sculpture of fine, crowded threads. Upper whorls usually have two large, crude spiral cords which gradually disappear on the body whorl. Aperture just less than half the length of the shell and somewhat flaring. This species is quite variable and has had many subspecies described. It is found offshore in deep water from Arctic Canada to Maine and in Scandinavia and the Shetland Islands.

Disreputable Neptune
3 in (7.5 cm)

New England Neptune, *Neptunea lyrata* subspecies *decemcostata* (Say, 1826). Broadly fusiform, solid. Characterized by its grayish white, rather smooth shell which bears seven to ten very strong, squarish, reddish brown, spiral cords. The upper whorls show two or three cords. There is an additional band of brown just below the suture. This is a common soft-bottom carnivore found offshore and distributed from off Nova Scotia to off North Carolina.

A form or possibly subspecies, *N. lyrata turnerae* A. H. Clarke, 1956, has a shorter spire and broader shell. It ranges from Grand Manan Island, New Brunswick, to Mount Desert Island, Maine.

New England Neptune
4 in (10 cm)

Clench's Neptune, *Neptunea despecta* subspecies *clenchi* A. H. Clarke, 1956. Similar to the Disreputable Neptune, but more elongate, with a higher spire and much stronger spiral cords. The siphonal canal is not as twisted although it is longer. It occurs along the northern Arctic areas of Canada.

Clench's Neptune
4 in (10 cm)

Phoenician Neptune, *Neptune lyrata* subspecies *phoenicea* (Dall, 1891). Elongate-fusiform, with five or six well-rounded whorls bearing numerous, small, raised, smooth, rounded spiral cords, seven on the upper whorls, twenty weaker ones on the body whorl. Color of shell a uniform taffy-brown with lighter cords and threads. Aperture ovate, a little greater than half the length of the shell, slightly flaring, and blending in below with the short broad siphonal canal. Columella and inside of aperture white. Commonly dredged off the northern coast of British Columbia.

Phoenician Neptune
4 in (10 cm)

Ventricose Neptune, *Neptunea ventricosa* (Gmelin, 1791). Shell fat, heavy and solid. The swollen last whorl may bear weak or strong, rounded slanting axial ribs. Columella strongly twisted to the right. The siphonal fasciole often with scale-like fimbriations. Color of shell a dirty-brownish white. Aperture white or flushed with brownish purple. Moderately common offshore. Ranges across the Arctic Ocean, especially in northern Alaska; also Scandinavia, northern Scotland and Iceland.

Ventricose Neptune
3.5 in (9 cm)

Ancient Neptune, *Neptunea antiqua* (Linnaeus, 1758). Large, strong shell, yellowish to gray, with weak, fine, spiral threads. Whorls rounded, swollen. Outer lip strong and smooth. Siphonal canal short, slightly twisted. A rare all-white form occurs in the North Sea. Sometimes specimens have a deep-orange mouth. Freaks may be sinistral. An edible species, common around the British Isles; Scandinavia and France; offshore to 6000 ft (1830 m).

Ancient Neptune
4 in (10 cm)

Contrary Neptune, *Neptunea contraria* (Linnaeus, 1771). Shell fusiform, sinistrally coiled, with a pointed spire, well-rounded whorls and a well-indented suture. Sculpture of numerous, crowded, squarish, raised, weakly beaded cords. Color of shell a rich light-brown with a white aperture and siphonal canal. Outer lip slightly flaring and slightly crenulated. Operculum half size of the aperture, brown, chitinous, with a terminal nucleus. Moderately common offshore species from Portugal south into the Mediterranean.

Contrary Neptune
3.5 in (9 cm)

Smirnia Neptune, *Neptunea smirnia* (Dall, 1919). Fusiform, fairly large, with a large, slightly flaring aperture which is greater than half the entire length of the shell. Surface smoothish, except for four or five very weak, low, flat spiral cords on the early whorls. Last two whorls smooth shouldered and with fine, faint, silky growth lines. Color tan with a brown-stained aperture. A common soft-bottom species in

Smirnia Neptune
3.5 in (9 cm)

330 to 985 ft (100–300 m) of water. Occurs from northern Japan to Alaska and south off Washington State.

Heros Neptune, *Neptunea heros* (Gray, 1850). Shell large, heavy, fusiform with the shoulders angled by an irregular spiral cord. Axial ribs subdued and irregular. One spiral cord is usually prominent on the middle of the upper whorls. Scales on siphonal fasciole. Color tawny-brown. Aperture whitish. Operculum chitinous, brown, almost as large as the aperture and its nucleus at the terminal end. Lives offshore in Arctic Seas from Japan to Alaska; uncommon.

Heros Neptune
4 in (10 cm)

Stiles Neptune, *Neptunea stilesi* A. G. Smith, 1968. Shell very broadly fusiform with a short spire and large last whorl. Outer lip not flaring. Siphonal canal relatively short. Columellar edge raised and glossy-white. Color of shell dingy-white to tan or yellowish and occasionally reddish brown. Major sculpturing of widely spaced, distinct, rounded, low spiral cords which are darker brown. Uncommon from 223 to 820 ft (68–250 m). Ranges from off Vancouver Island, British Columbia, to Washington.

Stiles Neptune
4 in (10 cm)

Tabled Neptune, *Neptunea tabulata* (Baird, 1863). Shell fusiform, solid, with eight white whorls covered with a thin, brown periostracum. Characterized by the wide, flat channel next to the suture. It is bounded by a raised, scaly or fimbriated spiral cord. Remainder of whorl with

Tabled Neptune
3 in (7.5 cm)

numerous sandpapery spiral threads. Aperture white and one third the length of the entire shell. Siphonal canal moderately long, and sometimes with a very small, narrow, chink-like umbilicus. Moderately common offshore from 195 to 1310 ft (60–400 m), extending from British Columbia to San Diego, California.

Kroyer's Colus, *Plicifusus kroyeri* (Moller, 1842). Shell fusiform, with about seven rounded whorls bearing numerous, distinct, rounded, axial ribs. Suture narrowly and deeply indented. Exterior covered with a shiny, olive-brown periostracum. Aperture round, slightly less than half the length of the shell. Outer lip thin, slightly flaring. Columella has a built-up, narrow callus, and is quite twisted at the lower end. An offshore circumpolar species from the Bering Sea and Greenland to Norway.

Kroyer's Colus
3 in (7.5 cm)

Fenestrate Colus, *Siphonorbis fenestratus* (Turton, 1834). Somewhat fusiform, with a high spire of about seven slightly convex whorls. White, ovate aperture about one third the length of the shell. Siphonal canal short, slightly twisted. Suture strongly indented. Sculpture in upper whorls of numerous, rounded axial plicae crossed by several, smaller spiral threads. Nuclear whorls large and smooth. Color of shell white. Animal creamy-white, siphon with many dark streaks. Alias *Turrisipho fusiformis* (Broderip, 1830), not Borson, 1820. Uncommon on gravel and sand bottoms. Ranges

Fenestrate Colus
1.6 in (4.5 cm)

from Newfoundland and Greenland to Scandinavia and rarely in the northern British Isles.

Ivory Colus, *Siphonorbis ebur* (Mörch, 1869). Similar to the Fenestrate Colus, but the spire is shorter, whorls more rounded, aperture about half the length of the shell, and lacking the axial ribs. Sculpture of numerous, irregularly placed, fine spiral threads crossed by even finer lines of growth. Siphonal canal short and slightly leaning to the left. Shell alabaster white. Inhabits Arctic waters of northwest Scandinavia and Iceland.

Ivory Colus
3 in (7.5 cm)

Howse's Colus, *Siphonorbis howsei* (Marshall, 1911). Shell fusiform, solid, white, smoothish, except for weak, irregular spiral threads. Aperture about half the length of the entire shell. Suture finely indented. Outer lip thin, strong and smooth. Columella arched, the siphonal canal usually twisted to the left. Periostracum thin, translucent yellowish. Occurs offshore from 115 to 558 ft (35–170 m) in northwest Europe.

Howse's Colus
1.5 in (4 cm)

Destiny Colus, *Turrisipho lachesis* (Mörch, 1869). Shell elongate-fusiform, with about eight very rounded whorls. Spire high; aperture small, about quarter the length of the entire shell. Siphonal canal relatively short and narrow. Suture well-impressed. Axial sculpture absent. Whorls covered by numerous, crowded, small, flattish spiral cords. Color of shell dirty-white; small aperture white

Destiny Colus
1.8 in (4.5 cm)

with a large brown, chitinous operculum. Periostracum, when present, is soft and gray. This uncommon carnivore lives on soft mud bottoms offshore in the area of Norway.

Ample Fragile Buccinum, *Volutharpa ampullacea* (Middendorff, 1848). Shell small, fragile, ovate and with a low spire. Aperture more than half the length of the shell; outer lip thin and flaring below. Siphonal canal short, its notch U-shaped. Nuclear whorl small and white. Four remaining whorls convex, smoothish. Color of shell cream with broad axial streaks of yellow-brown or purplish. Suture slightly channeled. Periostracum thin, fuzzy, and grayish green. This is a moderately common, cold-water species living on gravel bottoms. It ranges from the Bering Sea to off British Columbia.

Ample Fragile Buccinum
1.5 in (4 cm)

Kellet's Whelk, *Kelletia kelleti* (Forbes, 1850). Shell very heavy and solid, broadly fusiform with a fine, wavy suture and a sharp, crimped outer lip. Whorls slightly concave between the suture and the shouldered periphery. The latter bears ten strong, rounded, elevated knobs per whorl. Base with about six to ten incised, spiral lines. Aperture glossy and white. Very common from northern California to Mexico in subtidal, rocky areas, as well as in Japan.

Kellet's Whelk
4 in (10 cm)

Dire Whelk, *Searlesia dira* (Reeve, 1846). Shell small, solid, fusiform with an acute spire, bearing nine to eleven low, rounded axial ribs.

Spiral sculpture of numerous, unequal-sized spiral threads. Aperture slightly more than half the length of the shell and colored tan. Outer lip not flaring and made crenulate by the numerous, short, whitish spiral teeth just inside the aperture. Columella concave, thickened by an orange-brown, glossy callus. This is a common shallow-water species ranging from Alaska to Monterey, California.

Dire Whelk
1 in (2.5 cm)

Channeled Whelk, *Busycotypus canaliculatus* (Linnaeus, 1758). Shell fairly large, lightweight, fusiform with a relatively low spire and a large aperture that is three-quarters the length of the shell. Characterized by a deep, squarish, rather wide channel running along the suture. Periostracum heavy, felt-like and gray. The squarish shoulder is weakly beaded in the earlier whorls. Fairly common in shallow water from Cape Cod to northeastern Florida. Introduced to California prior to 1948.

Channeled Whelk
6 in (15 cm)

Harford's Spindle, *Fusinus harfordi* (Stearns, 1871). Shell of moderate size, fusiform, solid with a white aperture half the length of the shell. Exterior dark, orange-brown, with eleven or twelve wide, rounded ribs crossed by small, sharply raised, fine, scaled spiral cords. Inside of aperture with numerous, weak, white, spiral lirae. Siphonal canal moderately long. This genus belongs in the family Fasciolariidae. The species is uncommon off British Columbia to northern California.

Harford's Spindle
2 in (5 cm)

Nassa
Mud Snails
(*Family Nassariidae*)

These small sand- and mud-dwelling snails are common scavengers in most parts of the world, particularly in warm seas where there are large stretches of sand and mud flats left exposed at low tide. The operculum is chitinous, oval and usually with a serrated edge.

Eastern Mud Snail, *Ilyanassa obsoleta* (Say, 1822). A gregarious, abundant species on intertidal mud flats. Shell ovate, solid, smoothish with a high, slightly convex spire. Aperture one third the length of the shell. Color dark-brown with a narrow, tan, color band on the middle of the last whorl. Aperture chocolate-brown. Columella with a strong spiral tooth at the base. Ranges from Quebec to northeast Florida; introduced to British Columbia and California.

Eastern Mud Snail
0.8 in (2 cm)

Giant Western Nassa, *Nassarius fossatus* (Gould, 1849). One of the largest known nassas. Orange-brown to gray in color. Early whorls coarsely beaded; last whorl with about a dozen coarse, variously sized, flat-topped spiral threads and short axial riblets. A common intertidal species from Vancouver Island to Mexico.

Giant Western Nassa
1.5 in (4 cm)

Western Lean Nassa, *Nassarius mendicus* (Gould, 1849). Spire high. Sculpture of numerous, small beads. Common in shallow water from Alaska to California.

Western Lean Nassa
0.8 in (2 cm)

Western Fat Nassa, *Nassarius perpinquis* (Hinds, 1844). Fairly thin-shelled but strong, with a straight, acute spire and an aperture less than half the length of the shell. Outer lip fragile. Characterized by a neat beaded sculpture. Parietal wall glazed over with tan, while the remainder of the shell is yellowish brown. There is a small white tooth on the upper part of the inner wall. Columella arched and ending below with a single, spiral lira. Inside of outer lip with fine lirae. Abundant on intertidal flats to a depth of 330 ft (100 m) from Vancouver Island to Baja California.

Western Fat Nassa
1 in (2.5 cm)

Pygmy Nassa, *Nassarius pygmaeus* (Lamarck, 1822). Shell small, with an acute spire, swollen last whorl, strongly sculptured with axial ribs bearing round beads. Aperture small, ovate and encircled with a thick, beaded outer lip and arched, glossy columella. Base of columella with two whitish swellings. Nine or ten small teeth within the outer lip. Siphonal canal wide and with a gutter above it on the last whorl. Color brownish gray, sometimes with three subdued spiral bands. Uncommon just offshore to 655 ft (200 m) on sandy bottoms. Ranges from southern Norway, the Shetlands to the British Isles. Some workers place it in the genus, or subgenus, *Hinia*.

Pygmy Nassa
0.5 in (1.2 cm)

New England Nassa, *Nassarius trivittatus* (Say, 1822). Rather light-shelled, with eight or nine whorls which are slightly channeled below the suture. Apex acute. Spiral sculpture of four or five rows of strong, distinct beads. Parietal wall glazed with white enamel. Outer lip sharp and thin. Color yellowish gray. Lives in shallow water down to 230 ft (70 m) on sand. Common from Newfoundland to off northeast Florida.

New England Nassa
0.7 in (2 cm)

Common Eastern Nassa, *Nassarius vibex* (Say, 1822). Shell small, but solid, with a well-developed parietal shield. Last whorl with about a dozen, poorly developed, axial ribs which are coarsely beaded. Color gray-brown to whitish with a few blotches or broken bands of darker brown. Inside of outer lip with four or five enamel teeth, the largest at the top. Siphonal canal recurved; columella with two small spiral lirae at the base. Parietal shield sometimes yellowish. A common intertidal mudflat species ranging from southern Cape Cod to Florida, Texas and to Brazil.

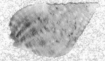

Common Eastern Nassa
0.5 in (1.2 cm)

Thickened Nassa, *Nassarius incrassatus* (Ström, 1768). A small, thick shell with an acute spire and small aperture surrounded by a thickened lip. Five whorls with ten to twelve rounded axial ribs crossed by numerous spiral ridges. Suture wavy. Parietal shield and outer lip enamel-white. Behind the lip is a swollen varix. Inside of outer lip with five or six small lirae. Color reddish buff to yellow-gray,

Thickened Nassa
0.5 in (1.2 cm)

sometimes with a subsutural darker band. Common in large colonies in muddy areas. Its range extends from most of western Europe into the Mediterranean. Belongs to the subgenus *Tritonella*.

Reticulated Nassa, *Nassarius reticulatus* (Linnaeus, 1758). Solid, heavy, coarse shell, quite variable in its sculpturing which may be coarsely beaded or with widely spaced, coarsely knobbed axial ribs. Suture well-indented and usually with a row of separate beads below it. Parietal wall well-callused. Color glossy-white with fine brown spiral lines and occasional dark blotches. These scavengers live in pockets of soft sand among rocky intertidal areas. The species is widely distributed from the Black Sea north to the British Isles and Norway.

Reticulated Nassa
1 in (2.5 cm)

✦

Olive Shells
(*Family Olividae*)

Although the glossy and attractive olive shells are associated with tropical waters, there are two species that have invaded the cooler waters of the Eastern Pacific. There is no operculum in the true *Oliva*, but some smaller *Olivella* have a chitinous one. All species are carnivorous scavengers. There are no olive shells in western Europe.

Purple Dwarf Olive, *Olivella biplicata* (Sowerby, 1825). Quite solid, globular-elongate. Upper columella wall with a heavy, white callus. Lower end of columella with a raised, spiral fold which is cut by two or three spiral, incised lines. Color bluish gray with violet stains around the fasciole and lower part of the aperture. Abundant in summer months in sandy bays and beaches. Ranges from Vancouver Island to Baja California.

Purple Dwarf Olive
1 in (2.5 cm)

Beatic Dwarf Olive, *Olivella baetica* Carpenter, 1864. Small, light-shelled, glossy and colored a drab-tan with weak purplish brown maculations arranged in axial flames. Fasciole white, often stained with brown. A moderately common, shallow-water sand species living from Kodiak Island, Alaska, to Baja California.

Beatic Dwarf Olive
0.5 in (1.2 cm)

False Greenland Mitre, *Volutomitra groenlandica* (Möller, 1842). Fusiform, solid, white with a dark-brown periostracum. Smoothish, the nuclear whorls smooth, the others with fine, spiral scratches. Minute axial riblets on the early whorls. Columella with four folds. Operculum chitinous. Uncommon; this offshore species belongs to the family Volutomitridae.

False Greenland Mitre
1 in (2.5 cm)

◆

Mitres and False Mitres
(*Families Mitridae and Volutomitridae*)

Both families are related, but their internal anatomy is different. The Volutomitridae are mainly cold-water dwellers, there being two from the Atlantic and one in the northwest Pacific. The Mitridae are mainly tropical. Both have two to four strong, oblique, spiral folds, or teeth, on the columella.

Alaskan False Mitre, *Volutomitra alaskana* Dall 1902. Fusiform, solid, resembling the False Greenland Mitre, but having a longer aperture and a thicker, smooth greenish brown periostracum. In both species the early whorls are badly eroded. A carnivorous species living in deep water from Pribilof Islands, Alaska, to off San Diego, California.

Alaskan False Mitre
1.5 in (4 cm)

Ebony Mitre, *Mitra ebenus* (Lamarck, 1811). Fusiform, solid, smooth, with slightly convex whorls and an indented suture. Aperture slightly more than half the length of the shell. Surface smooth, with about ten low, rounded ribs. Color blackish brown. Upper third of the last whorl with a narrow spiral band of tan. Columella with two large and two small, slanting folds. Outer lip thickened and with tiny teeth on the inner edge. Moderately

Ebony Mitre
1.2 in (3 cm)

common in rock pools in Mediterranean and Portugal.

Little Trumpet Mitre, *Mitra cornicula* (Linnaeus, 1758). Similar to the Ebony Mitre, but with smaller, weaker columella folds, a smooth outer lip, and with about seven or eight spiral threads on the base of the shell. Lacks ribs. Color glossy brown. A common littoral species of the Mediterranean extending to the Azores and to Portugal.

Little Trumpet Mitre
0.7 in (2 cm)

Volutes and Cones
(*Families Volutidae and Conidae*)

These two major families are poorly represented in northern waters. Only one volute exists in the cold waters of the north Pacific, and the only volute in western Europe is the Spotted Flask. Many hundreds of cones live in the warm waters of the world, but only the Mediterranean Cone comes as far north as Portugal.

Stearns' Volute, *Arctomelon stearnsi* (Dall, 1872). Shell large, fusiform, strong; the exterior chalky-gray with mauve-brown undertones. Aperture semi-glossy and light-brown . Nuclear whorls bulbous, smooth, but often eroded away. Columella brownish and with two large folds and a third

Stearns' Volute
4 in (10 cm)

weaker one below. Locally common offshore in Alaska.

Spotted Flask, *Ampulla priamus* (Gmelin, 1791). Shell oval, thin-shelled but strong, with only three or four convex whorls. Smooth, shiny, light-brown with six distantly placed rows of small, round dots of reddish brown on the last whorl. Outer lip thin and sharp. No operculum. Frequently dredged in fairly deep water off Spain and Portugal. *Halia* is a synonym.

Spotted Flask
2.5 in (6.5 cm)

Mediterranean Cone, *Conus ventricosus* (Gmelin, 1791) . Shell elongate-conic, solid, with a short, flattish spire and straight sides, with weak spiral incised lines at the base. Color variable, but usually a dull-brown or maculated or with a light spiral band at the middle. Base of the outer lip with a brown edge. A common Mediterranean shallow-water cone also found in Portugal.

Mediterranean Cone
1 in (2.5 cm)

Turrids
(*Family Turridae*)

This is a very large, worldwide family with hundreds of genera and thousands of species, thus making it a difficult group to identify without extensive, well-illustrated monographs. Most are fusiform and rather small, with a slit, notch or U-shaped canal at the top of the outer lip, known as the "turrid" notch. Operculum chitinous.

Slender Mangelia, *Mangelia gracilis* (Montagu, 1803). Shell evenly fusiform, with a high, acute spire. Whorls nine, bearing ten to fourteen rounded axial ribs which are on the upper third of the last whorl. Spiral sculpture of minute threads overriding the ribs. Outer lip sharp, thickened behind by a swollen varix, and with a small, but deep "turrid" notch. Color cream with yellow banding. Occurs on gravel bottoms from 23 to 492 ft (7–150 m) from the Mediterranean to the southern British Isles.

Slender Mangelia
0.8 in (2 cm)

Incised Drillia, *Ophiodermella incisa* (Carpenter, 1865). Fusiform, solid; covered with numerous, spiral cut lines. "Turrid notch" very shallow and weak. Periostracum brownish. Operculum chitinous with a terminal nucleus. Common offshore from Puget Sound to California.

Incised Drillia
0.5 in (1.2 cm)

Goode's Aforia, *Aforia goodei* (Dall, 1890). Shell fairly large, lightweight, fusiform and chalky white. There is a strong, spiral cord on the shoulder of the whorls. Above it are axial growth scars showing the former "turrid notches." Common from off British Columbia to southern Chile.

Goode's Aforia
3.5 in (9 cm)

Bubble Shells

(*Families Acteonidae and Scaphandridae*)

The great snail subclass Opisthobranchia contains a vast number of diverse hermaphrodites that includes the naked seaslugs, or nudibranchs, and the bubble shells with their very delicate, coiled shells. Most lack an operculum, with the exception of *Acteon*.

Lathe Acteon, *Acteon tornatilis* (Linnaeus, 1758). Shell broadly fusiform, solid, with a convex spire and long aperture three-quarters the length of the entire shell. Sculpture of numerous, very fine, spiral incised lines becoming stronger towards the base of the shell. Color pinkish yellow with three lighter spiral bands, two being bordered by a dark-brown line. Operculum chitinous. Occurs offshore from Iceland to Spain.

Lathe Acteon
0.5 in (1.2 cm)

Giant Canoe-bubble, *Scaphander punctostriatus* Mighels, 1841. Shell lightweight, ovate-oblong. Apex with a slightly sunken area. Aperture constricted above, the outer lip projecting above the apex. Shell smoothish, except for numerous, spiral rows of microscopic, elongate punctations. Color chalk-white, with a straw periostracum. Moderately common offshore on sand. Ranges

Giant Canoe-bubble
1.5 in (3.5 cm)

from the Arctic Seas to Florida;
Greenland and Iceland,
uncommon.

Wooden Canoe-bubble,
Scaphander lignarius (Linnaeus,
1758). Shell solid, opaque, ovate-
oblong, with the upper half
constricted. Exterior cream, with
numerous, fine spiral scratches and
brown lines. Color variable from
yellow to brownish green. A
common sublittoral sand-dwelling
species. It ranges from the British
Isles to the Mediterranean and the
Canary Islands.

Wooden Canoe-bubble
1 in (2.5 cm)

Open Paper-bubble, *Philine
aperta* (Linnaeus, 1767). Shell
fragile, translucent, oval, with a
very large, wide aperture. Outer lip
projects above the apex. Pale-
yellow animal covers the shell. The
skin is capable of secreting a
protective layer of sulphuric acid.
Within the stomach of all *Philine*
are three solid, flat gizzard plates.
It lives on sandy bottoms and
preys upon small molluscs and
polychaete worms. This is a
common offshore species ranging
from Norway to the
Mediterranean, as well as South
Africa and the Indian Ocean.

Open Paper-bubble
1.5 in (4 cm)

Gould's Paper-bubble,
Haminoea vesicula Gould, 1855.
Shell very fragile, globular,
translucent yellow, with a thin
rusty brown or yellowish orange
periostracum. There is a very small
perforation at the concealed apex.
Similar to *H. virescens*, but the
body whorl is larger, the aperture
smaller and the columella
thickened at the base and forming

Gould's Paper-bubble
0.7 in (2 cm)

an indented umbilicus. Belongs in
the family Haminoeidae. A
common, littoral bay species
ranging from southern Alaska to
the Gulf of California.

Sowerby's Paper-bubble,
Haminoea virescens (Sowerby,
1833). Shell, fragile, globular and
translucent greenish yellow in
color. Aperture very large and
open. Upper part of the outer lip
high and narrowly winged. No
apical hole. The animal is dark-
green with yellowish markings:
dots on the head shield, mottlings
on the parapodia. A common,
shallow-water species of the open
coast. It prefers sandy areas where
there are beds of seagrass where it
lays small gelatinous egg masses on
the stems of weeds. Found from
Puget Sound, Washington, to the
Gulf of California.

Sowerby's Paper-bubble
0.5 in (1.2 cm)

Solitary Paper-bubble,
Haminoea solitaria (Say, 1822).
Shell fragile, oblong, with the
aperture as long as the entire shell.
Apertural lip arising on the right
side of the apical perforation.
Spiral sculpture of numerous, very
fine scratches. Color translucent
amber to whitish. Prefers a shallow
sandy area where there are
protective grasses. It lays its
gelatinous egg masses on the stems
of weeds. This is a common,
carnivorous species distributed
from Cape Cod, Massachusetts, to
off North Carolina.

Solitary Paper-bubble
0.5 in (1.2 cm)

Watery Paper-bubble,
Haminoea hydatis (Linnaeus,
1758). Shell fragile, globular,
inflated, translucent white or

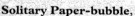

yellowish, with the aperture slightly longer than the spire. Columella thickened with a white glaze. Exterior surface smooth, except for fine, irregular growth lines. Soft parts light-brown and cover most of the shell. The anterior cephalic disc bears two small black eyes on the dorsal surface. This species feeds on small bivalves. It occurs in muddy sand in subtidal areas from the British Isles to the Mediterranean.

Watery Paper-bubble
0.5 in (1.2 cm)

Bubble Akera, *Akera bullata* Müller, 1776. Shell fragile, globular and the whorls enrolled at the apex. The shell is carried externally at the hind end of an elongate animal which has two elongate parapodia extending over the back of the animal and part of the shell. Lacks tentacles. Soft parts pale-gray to orange, with many small white and black spots and streaks. A purple fluid may be secreted if the animal is disturbed. It is capable of swimming by flapping its parapodia. This carnivore lives in sandy and weedy areas and serves as a food for flounders. It ranges from Norway, throughout the British Isles, south into the Mediterranean.

Bubble Akera
0.7 in (2 cm)

Sea Butterflies
(*Order Pteropoda*)

The world's oceans are heavily populated with these small, abundant snails that live near the surface and form a large part of the planktonic hordes upon which most life in the seas depends, particularly some species of whales and oceanic fishes. The shells are delicate, glassy and translucent. There are fifteen genera and about a hundred species, most with a worldwide distribution in both cold and warm seas.

Uncinate Cavoline, *Cavolinia uncinata* (Rang, 1829). Shell small, glassy, translucent and brownish. Dorsal lip with a thin margin. Ventral lip not more developed than the dorsal one. Shell with distinct lateral points. Upper lip flattened posteriorly. This is usually a warm-water, pelagic species found in the Atlantic as far north as Newfoundland and Alaska. There are five common species in this genus.

Uncinate Cavoline
0.5 in (1.2 cm)

Pyramid Clio, *Clio pyramidata* Linnaeus, 1767. Shell of an angular form, compressed, colorless and with lateral keels. A cross-section of the front end is always angular at the sides. There is usually a ridge extending longitudinally along the back. Surface with wavy ribs. A worldwide pelagic species and popular food of whales.

Pyramid Clio
0.7 in (2 cm)

Cigar Pteropod, *Cuvierina columnella* (Rang, 1827). Shell small, cylindrical, shaped somewhat like a fat cigar. Surface smooth. A cross-section is almost circular. Behind the aperture there is a slight constriction. This is the only species in the genus.

Cigar Pteropod
0.4 in (1 cm)

TUSK
SHELLS

Tusk Shells
(*Class Scaphopoda*)

This group of sand-dwelling molluscs is worldwide in distribution, but has fewer than a thousand species. The shell is open at both ends. The narrow end protrudes above the sandy bottom where water is drawn in and expelled at alternating intervals. At the large end, the conic-shaped foot and dozens of ciliated, prehensile threads project through the sand. Tusk shells feed upon single-celled foraminifera. Identification depends upon the nature of the slits at the small end of the shell and in the nature of the ribbing.

Wampum Tusk, *Antalis pretiosum* (Sowerby, 1860). Moderately curved and solid; opaque-white, ivory-like, commonly with faint dirty-yellow rings of growth. Apex with a short notch on the convex side. A common offshore species living in sandy mud. It was used extensively as money by the northwest Indian tribes. It ranges from Alaska to Baja California.

Wampum Tusk
2 in (5 cm)

Western Straight Tusk, *Laevidentalium rectius* (Carpenter, 1864). Almost straight, slender and long and attenuated towards the apex. Thin-shelled and fragile. Surface glossy and smoothish. Color bluish white, somewhat translucent, with some opaque-white flecks and rings. Apical opening without a notch. Moderately common offshore from Alaska to Panama.

Western Straight Tusk
1.2 in (3 cm)

Western Atlantic Tusk, *Antalis occidentale* (Stimpson, 1851). Sixteen to eighteen primary ribs, fairly distinct in the young stages. Sculptureless in the senile stage. Round in cross-section. Common offshore from Newfoundland to off North Carolina.

Western Atlantic Tusk
1.2 in (3 cm)

Entale Tusk, *Antalis entalis* (Linnaeus, 1758). Moderately curved, solid, round in cross-section and finely striate longitudinally. Color ivory-white, sometimes with a rusty stain on the narrow end, caused by a mixture of mud and sand in which it burrows. Margin of larger end often jagged. Small end with a very short, oblique pipe or tubular appendage having a pear-shaped opening. This is a common, sand-dwelling, offshore species found in Arctic waters from Nova Scotia to Massachusetts; and from Iceland and Norway south to off Portugal.

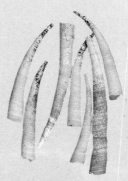

Entale Tusk
2 in (5 cm)

Common Tusk, *Antalis vulgaris* (da Costa, 1778). Moderately curved, solid and wide. Circular in cross-section. Opaque-white, sometimes tinted with yellowish brown or rose towards the narrow, apical end. Sculpture of fine, crowded longitudinal striae, about thirty at the apex. Aperture oblique, thin and jagged. Anal opening small, round or ovate and occupying a very short tube. No notch or slit present. Common offshore in muddy and sandy areas from southern England and Ireland southward into the Mediterranean.

Common Tusk
2 in (5 cm)

European Tusk, *Dentalium dentale* Linnaeus, 1766.
Moderately curved, rather slender. Opaque-white, sometimes suffused with rose at the smaller end. Sculpture of about ten strong, rounded, longitudinal ribs near the apex, becoming eighteen to twenty near the aperture. Aperture rounded, polygonal, slightly oblique. Anal orifice small, circular and with very thick walls. No notch or slit present. This is a southern species living offshore from Portugal south into the Mediterranean and the Adriatic.

European Tusk
1 in (2.5 cm)

◆

THE
CHITONS

Chitons
(*Class Polyplacophora*)

These rock-dwelling, elongate molluscs have eight shelly plates bound together at the sides by a leathery girdle which may be smooth, hairy or covered with small, shelly scales. The flat foot occupies most of the underside, with the small head possessing a mouth with radular teeth, but without tentacles or eyes. There are about 600 species throughout the world.

Northern Red Chiton, *Tonicella rubra* (Linnaeus, 1767). Oblong, moderately elevated, and with the valves rather rounded. Upper surfaces smooth, except for fine growth wrinkles. Colored light-tan over which are orange-red marblings. Interior of valves bright pink. Girdle reddish brown, covered with minute, elongate, separate scales. Common on hard surfaces from 9 to 656 ft (3–200 m). Arctic Seas to Connecticut; also Bering Strait to northern California; Norway to Portugal.

Northern Red Chiton
1 in (2.5 cm)

Mottled Red Chiton, *Tonicella marmorea* (Fabricius, 1780). Oblong to oval, elevated, and rather sharply angular. Upper surface smoothish and with microscopic granulations. Interior of valves tinted with rose. Girdle leathery and without scales or bristles. Common from 9 to 328 ft (3–100 m). Greenland to Massachusetts; Japan and Alaska to Washington State; Norway to the British Isles.

Mottled Red Chiton
1 in (2.5 cm)

Lined Red Chiton, *Tonicella lineata* (Wood, 1815). Valves shiny smooth, orange to deep red with oblique black lines bordered with white. Interior of valves white. Girdle naked. Common in shallow water from Japan to Alaska to northern California.

Lined Red Chiton
1.2 in (3 cm)

Mertens' Chiton, *Lepidozona mertensii* (Middendorff, 1847). Oval in shape; color variable: commonly yellowish with dark reddish brown streaks and maculations. Central areas of the valves with strong, longitudinal ribs and smaller, cross ridges which give a netted appearance. Anterior valve with thirty or more radial rows of tiny warts. Interior of valves whitish. Girdle with alternating yellow and reddish bands, and covered with tiny, low, smooth, split-pea scales. Abundant in shallow water on hard surfaces. Ranges from the Aleutian Islands to Baja California, Mexico.

Mertens' Chiton
1.5 in (4 cm)

Mossy Mopalia, *Mopalia muscosa* (Gould, 1846). Oblong to oval. Head valve with ten beaded ribs. Color usually a dull-brown, blackish olive or grayish. Interior of valves blue-green, rarely stained pinkish. Girdle with stiff hairs resembling a fringe of moss. Many varieties were described. This is a common intertidal species ranging along the entire coast from Alaska to Baja California, Mexico.

Mossy Mopalia
1.5 in (4 cm)

Eastern American Chiton, *Chaetopleura apiculata* (Say, 1830). Small, oblong to oval. Valves slightly carinate. Central area of valves with fifteen to twenty longitudinal rows of raised, neat beads. Lateral areas distinctly defined, raised, and bearing numerous, larger beads. Interior of valves white or grayish. Girdle narrow, mottled cream and brown, and microscopically granulose and sparsely scattered with short, transparent hairs. This common species is usually found attached to small rocks and to dead shells in shallow water. It ranges from Cape Cod, Massachusetts, to both sides of Florida.

Eastern American Chiton
0.8 in (2 cm)

THE
BIVALVES

The Bivalves
(*Class Bivalvia*)

The class Bivalvia or Pelecypoda includes such molluscs as the
clams, oysters and scallops. There are about 10,000 living
species, most living in the world's seas, but many are found only
in freshwater rivers and lakes. The soft parts lack a true head
and radular teeth, and are protected by two shelly valves, hence
the name "bivalves." Locomotion is accomplished by a tongue-
like foot that protrudes from the front end. Some species, like
the oysters, become permanently attached to the substrate. At
the rear are two fleshy, tube-like siphons, sometimes fused into
one, through which water is inhaled or exhaled. Microscopic
forms of vegetable matter are drawn in over the mucus-covered
gills and passed into a small mouth. In most clams the sexes are
in separate individuals, but a few are hermaphroditic or can
change sex periodically. Eggs are sometimes brooded within the
gills or may be shed into the open sea where released sperm can
fertilize them. The larval or veliger forms of bivalves float and
swim freely, sometimes for many miles before they settle down
on the bottom and change into shelly bivalves. Bivalves may
have a life span of two to one hundred years.
   The valves of bivalves are held together by one or two
adductor muscles, and are kept ajar by a chitinous, elastic
ligament which may sometimes be located internally between
the teeth of the hinge. The shape and number of hinge teeth,
the outline of the muscle scars on the inside of the valves, and
the exterior sculpturing are used in identifying the various
species.

Awning Clams
(*Family Solemyacidae*)

This is a relatively obscure and primitive-looking group of bivalves living in mud in U-shaped burrows that are open at each end. The oblong, cigar-shaped shells lack hinge teeth and are covered with a glossy, thin, brown periostracum which extends well beyond the margins of the shell. The foot is large and sucker-like at the broadened, flat end. The short siphonal opening is bordered by fleshy, tentacle-like appendages. The ligament is internal and near the posterior beak end. These clams harbour symbiotic bacteria to reduce sulphur oxides. The family appears to be absent in northwestern Europe.

Boreal Awning Clam, *Solemya borealis* Totten, 1834. Shell fragile, oblong, somewhat compressed laterally and with a glossy, rayed, chestnut-brown periostracum. Interior of valves grayish blue. Siphonal opening with three pairs of long tentacles on the upper part, and fifteen smaller ones bordering the lower half. Moderately common offshore from Nova Scotia to Connecticut.

Boreal Awning Clam
2.5 in (6.5 cm)

Atlantic Awning Clam, *Solemya velum* Say, 1822. Shell small; periostracum glossy light-brown with lighter radial rays of yellowish. Chondrophore supported by two curved arms. Siphonal opening with two pairs of small tubercles above, and five or six pairs of short tentacles below. A common, shallow-water species

Atlantic Awning Clam
1 in (2.5 cm)

ranging from Nova Scotia to northern Florida.

Toga Awning Clam, *Solemya togata* (Poli, 1795). Shell fragile; periostracum reddish brown with lighter rays. Offshore in mud from Portugal to West Africa and the Mediterranean.

Toga Awning Clam
2 in (5 cm)

Nut Clams
(*Family Nuculidae*)

These small clams have been abundant since the earliest development of bivalves during the Ordovician, 500 million years ago. They are characterized by their pearly interior and numerous, small "taxodont" teeth in the hinge. Below the beaks is a chitinous resilium set in a cup, or chondrophore. There is no pallial sinus scar. The shell's edge is crenulated in some species. Nut clams are distributed worldwide and are well-represented in cold waters, serving as food for bottom fish.

Atlantic Nut Clam, *Nucula proxima* Say, 1822. Very small, solid, obliquely ovate, smooth. Color greenish gray with microscopic, embedded, axial, gray lines and prominent, irregular, brownish, concentric rings. Outer shell overcast with an oily iridescence. Ventral edge minutely crenulate. A common, shallow-water species found in

Atlantic Nut Clam
0.3 in (7 mm)

sand and mud. Ranges from Nova Scotia to Florida and to Texas.

Smooth Nut Clam, *Nucula tenuis* (Montagu, 1808). Shell very small, ovate, smooth, except for irregular growth lines. Color a shiny, olive-green, sometimes with darker lines of growth. No radial lines present. Ventral edge smooth. Moderately common offshore in Arctic Seas, south to Florida; south to Spain; Japan to Alaska and south to California.

Smooth Nut Clam
0.2 in (5 mm)

Nuclear Nut Clam, *Nucula nucleus* (Linnaeus, 1758). Shell small, ovate; beaks behind midline; triangular in outline. Ventral edge crenulate. Common offshore from Norway to Africa; Labrador to Florida; Alaska to Mexico.

Nuclear Nut Clam
0.4 in (1 cm)

Pointed Nut Clams
(*Family Nuculanidae*)

These nut clams have a porcellaneous, rather than pearly, shell, and are usually rather drawn out or pointed at the posterior end. The chondrophore cup between the rows of taxodont teeth is usually rather large. The shells may have a prominent and deep pallial sinus. Most of these clams live offshore in cold waters.

Pointed Nut Clam, *Nuculana acuta* (Conrad, 1831). Shell very small, solid, rounded at the front end, pointed at the rear. Apex of the pallial sinus is broadly U-shaped. Concentric ribs evenly sized and evenly spaced extend over the rib which borders the dorsal surface of the pointed end. Color white with a thin, yellowish periostracum. This is a common, shallow-water species ranging from Cape Cod to Brazil.

Pointed Nut Clam
0.3 in (7 mm)

Fossa Nut Clam, *Nuculana fossa* (Baird, 1863). Shell elongate, moderately fat and smoothish, except for small, pronounced, concentric ribs at the anterior end and on the beaks. Dorsal area of rostrum is smoothish, depressed and bounded by two weak radial ribs. Found in sand at 3 to 459 ft (1–140 m) from Alaska to Puget Sound, Washington .

Fossa Nut Clam
1 in (2.5 cm)

Almond Yoldia, *Yoldia amygdalea* Valenciennes, 1846. Shell thin, compressed laterally, elongate and narrowing at the posterior end. The anterior ventral margin has a small concave depression. Moderately common in Arctic Seas to California, the Gulf of Maine, and to Norway.

Almond Yoldia
2 in (5 cm)

Ark
Clams
(*Family Arcidae*)

Ark shells are distributed in most warm-water seas around the world, with only a few extending into cooler waters. The oblong, sturdy shells are characterized by a straight hinge bearing many, small, interlocking "taxodont" teeth. In the true arks, there is a natural gape in the ventral edge of the shell through which passes the foot that spins a strong cluster of byssal threads.

Four-sided Ark, *Arca tetragona* Poli, 1795. Shell solid, box-shaped, with the widely separated beaks in the front half of the shell. There is a wide ventral gape where the massive, green byssus protrudes. Exterior finely reticulated and dirty white to yellowish with a brown periostracum. Ligament in a number of grooves radiating from the beaks across the cardinal area. Hinge plate straight, with forty to fifty small, similar teeth. Common in shallow water from Norway to the Mediterranean and Azores.

Four-sided Ark
1.3 in (3 cm)

Transverse Ark, *Anadara transversa* (Say, 1822). Shell solid, quadrate-oval; left valve overlaps the right valve. Thirty to thirty-five ribs per valve, those on the left valve usually beaded. Ligament long, narrow and pustulose. Fairly common in mud below low tide mark. Ranges from Cape Cod to Florida and to Texas.

Transverse Ark
1 in (2.5 cm)

Blood Ark, *Anadara ovalis*
(Bruguière, 1789). Shell fat and
oval, white, with twenty-six to
thirty-five smooth ribs. Ligament
very narrow and depressed; beaks
close together. Periostracum
blackish brown, hairy and fairly
thick. Flesh and blood are red. A
common shallow-water ark found
from Cape Cod to Texas.

Blood Ark
2 in (5 cm)

Milky Ark, *Arcopsis lactea*
(Linnaeus, 1767). Shell small,
solid, rhomboidal in outline;
somewhat compressed. Beaks just
in front of the mid-line and far
apart. Hinge plate with forty to
fifty small teeth. Exterior yellowish
white, with a light-brown
periostracum, sometimes
overhanging the margins.
Sculpture of fine radiating ribs
crossed by concentric ridges.
Interior whitish; muscle scars
raised. A common intertidal
species attached to rocks in sandy
areas. Ranges from the southern
coast of Britain to the
Mediterranean and to South
Africa.

Milky Ark
0.5 in (1.2 cm)

Nodulose Ark, *Acar nodulosa*
(Müller, 1776). Shell small, solid,
elongate-rhomboidal, with a
narrower front end and a broader,
spathate hind end. Beaks nearer
the smaller front end and set
slightly apart. Ligament long,
narrow and arrow-shaped. Hinge
with about seven teeth in front,
and about twelve slanting ones at
the posterior end. Sculpture of
worn reticulation and beads.
Periostracum thin and light-
brown. Interior of valves white.
Byssal gape very small. A common

Nodulose Ark
0.5 in (1.2 cm)

offshore and deepwater species ranging from Norway to Portugal.

Sulcate Limopsis, *Limopsis sulcata* Verrill and Bush, 1898. Shell small, obliquely oval, with prominent, rounded ribs which are finely cut on the upper edge by short, radial grooves. Inner margin of the valves smooth. Color dull-white. Periostracum thick, tufted, extending beyond the ventral edge of the shell. Hinge arched, with about six small teeth on either side of the center. Ligament external, small, central and triangular. Moderately common in sand offshore to a depth of about 2,296 ft (700 m). Ranges from Cape Cod to Texas and the West Indies. Belongs to the family Limopsidae.

Sulcate Limopsis
0.5 in (1.2 cm)

✦

Bittersweet Clams and Date Mussels
(*Families Glycymerididae and Mytilidae*)

The sturdy, oval, bittersweet clams of the family Glycymerididae have an arched hinge with a few taxodont teeth. The exterior is either smooth or strongly ribbed. Among the family Mytilidae are several species of date mussels that are adapted for boring by means of carbonic acid and shell rotation.

West Coast Bittersweet,
Glycymeris subobsoleta (Carpenter, 1864). Shell solid, compressed laterally, slightly longer than high, and chalky white with brownish markings. Periostracum velvety, but usually worn away. Radial ribs, flat with narrow interspaces. About nine short, elongate teeth on either side of the center of the hinge. Ventral edge with white teeth and brown coloring between. Moderately common just offshore to 26 ft (8 m) from the Aleutians to southern California.

West Coast Bittersweet
1 in (2.5 cm)

European Bittersweet,
Glycymeris glycymeris (Linnaeus, 1758). Shell solid, beaks central; almost circular in outline. Color yellow-brown, sometimes with irregular zigzag patterns. With very fine concentric and radiating lines. Very common offshore to 229 ft (70 m) on sandy gravel bottoms from Norway to the Mediterranean and Canary Islands.

European Bittersweet
2.5 in (6 cm)

European Date Mussel,
Lithophaga lithophaga (Linnaeus, 1758). Elongate, cigar-shaped. Umbo at the narrow anterior end. Exterior light-brown with fine growth lines. Interior bluish white. No hinge teeth. Bores in shallow-water rocks. Portugal to the Mediterranean and Adriatic Seas.

European Date Mussel
2.7 in (7 cm)

✦

Eastern American Oyster,
Crassostrea virginica (Gmelin,
1791). The valve margins are only
slightly wavy or are straight. Lower
valve cupped. The muscle scar is
usually colored a deep purple.
Harvested commercially along the
east coast of North America.

**Eastern American
Oyster**
5 in (12.5 cm)

Common European Oyster,
Ostrea edulis Linnaeus, 1758. Shell
roughly circular in outline.
Exterior rough, with deep radiating
ribs and concentric ridges. Upper
or right valve flat and brownish.
Interior whitish with green or red-
brown blotches. Common offshore
from Norway to the Black Sea

**Common European
Oyster**
4 in (10 cm)

Lucine
Clams
(*Family Lucinidae*)

These circular, laterally compressed clams are recognized by the
very long, narrow anterior muscle scar. The clams have very
short siphons and hence there is no pallial sinus. The long foot
is used to create a tunnel in the sandy mud for drawing in water
to the gills.

Northeast Lucina, *Lucinoma
filosa* (Stimpson, 1851). Almost
circular, compressed, white, with a
thin yellowish periostracum. Beaks
small, close together and centrally
located. No anterior lateral teeth
present. Sculpture of sharp,

Northeast Lucina
2.5 in (6.5 cm)

concentric ridges. Common offshore from Newfoundland to north Florida and to Texas.

Western Ringed Lucina, *Lucinoma annulata* (Reeve, 1850). Oval to circular and slightly inflated, with strong raised, concentric threads. Color chalky-gray to white, overlaid by a thin, greenish brown periostracum. Fairly common from 52 to 492 ft (16–150 m) from Alaska to southern California.

Western Ringed Lucina
2 in (5 cm)

Boreal Lucina, *Lucinoma borealis* (Linnaeus, 1758). Almost circular, solid, white with a thin brown periostracum. Strong concentric ridges are sometimes eroded away. Two small cardinal teeth in each valve. One of them is bifid. Margin of valves smooth. Lives in shallow water to 328 ft (100 m) in sandy mud. Ranges from Norway to the Baltic and south to the Mediterranean.

Boreal Lucina
1.2 in (3 cm)

Cardita and Astarte Clams
(*Families Carditidae and Astartidae*)

These families of small, solid clams serve as a major source of food for Arctic bottom-feeding fish. The clams are usually ovate, with the beaks near the center, and with a thick, dark-brown periostracum. There is no pallial sinus scar.

Fine-ribbed Cardita, *Cyclocardia borealis* (Conrad, 1831). Shell strong and obliquely heart-shaped. Beaks elevated and turned forward. Has about twenty rounded, moderately rough or beaded radial ribs. Color white, but usually covered with a thick, velvety brownish periostracum. Lunule small but very deeply sunk. A common offshore species ranging from Labrador to off North Carolina.

Fine-ribbed Cardita
1 in (2.5 cm)

Smooth Astarte, *Astarte castanea* (Say, 1822). Shell solid, fairly small, trigonal in outline and quite compressed. Beaks pointed and hooked forward. Lunule large and shallow. Exterior smoothish. Color a glossy light-brown. Inner margins finely crenulate. This is a common offshore species ranging from Nova Scotia to off New Jersey.

Smooth Astarte
1 in (2.5 cm)

Sulcate Astarte, *Astarte sulcata* (da Costa, 1778). Shell oval, slightly compressed, with twenty-four to fifty-five prominent, broad radial ribs. Lunule and escutcheon prominent. Inner margin finely crenulate. Periostracum light-brown. Color of shell white to salmon-pink. Common offshore from Greenland and Iceland to the Mediterranean.

Sulcate Astarte
1 in (2.5 cm)

✦

Cockles
(*Family Cardiidae*)

The well-known cockle family is worldwide in distribution and contains several dozen genera and several hundred living species. The shells vary from the large and copious *Cardium* of West Africa to the flat, heart-shaped *Corculum* of the East Indies. The foot of the cockles is large and muscular and the siphons are quite short. The ligament is external.

European Spiny Cockle, *Acanthocardia aculeata* (Linnaeus, 1767). Thin-shelled but strong, broadly oval in outline and with twenty to twenty-two strong, radial ribs, each bearing a row of spines down the middle. Right valve with two anterior laterals and one posterior lateral. Interior of valves radially furrowed. Color yellowish brown, with darker blotches. Subtidal to 98 ft (30 m). Rare in Britain; commoner southward into the Mediterranean.

European Spiny Cockle
3 in (7.5 cm)

Sand Cockle, *Acanthocardia spinosa* (Lightfoot, 1786). Broadly oval, with about thirty-five small, squarish radial ribs, those at the anterior end bearing smooth, rounded scales, and those at the posterior end having numerous, short spines. Color yellow-brown. A Mediterranean species ranging north to Portugal.

Tuberculate Cockle, *Acanthocardia tuberculata* (Linnaeus, 1758). Elongate-oval, with the beaks near the anterior

Sand Cockle
2.5 in (6.5 cm)

end. Twenty-one to twenty-three weakly beaded radial ribs. Color light brown. A common shallow-water cockle from the British Isles to the Mediterranean.

Morton's Egg Cockle, *Laevicardium mortoni* (Conrad, 1830). Thin-shelled, small, swollen and oval. Surface smooth, glossy, yellowish brown with darker zigzag markings and with fine concentric ridges which may be minutely pimpled. This common food for ducks lives in sand from 3 to 19 ft (1–6 m) of water. It ranges from Cape Cod to Texas.

Heavy Egg Cockle, *Laevicardium crassum* (Gmelin, 1791). Shell solid, obliquely oval, with the beaks well in front of the midline. Color dirty yellow, sometimes with red and brown blotches and zigzag markings, especially near the beaks. Periostracum thin, greenish yellow. Sculpture of forty to fifty very faint, smooth radial riblets. No spines or scales. Interior cream-tan. Margins crenulate. This common species lives among broken shell and gravel from Norway to the Mediterranean and the Cape Verde Islands.

Greenland Cockle, *Serripes groenlandicus* (Bruguière, 1789). Shell fairly large, solid, inflated, and with a slight gape at the pointed posterior end. Exterior smoothish, brownish gray. Interior dull-white. Beaks inflated. Ligament large and strong. No lunule or pallial sinus. Foot of

Tuberculate Cockle
2.5 in (6.5 cm)

Morton's Egg Cockle
1 in (2.5 cm)

Heavy Egg Cockle
3 in (7.5 cm)

animal mottled red. Common offshore from 19 to 393 ft (6–120 m) in Arctic Seas to Massachusetts and to Puget Sound, Washington State.

Nuttall's Cockle, *Clinocardium nuttallii* (Conrad, 1837). Shell fairly large, roundly oval, moderately compressed and usually with thirty-three to thirty-seven coarse, radial ribs with half-moon beads. Older specimens are worn smooth. Beaks nearer the anterior end and considerably rolled in. Interior whitish, with the margins showing distinct ribbing. Color drab-gray, with a thin, brownish yellow periostracum. A common offshore sand-loving cockle ranging from the Bering Sea and Alaska to off southern California.

Iceland Cockle, *Clinocardium ciliatum* (Fabricius, 1780). Fairly large, roundly oval, moderately compressed, with thirty-two to thirty-eight ridged radial ribs which are crossed by coarse, concentric lines of growth. Exterior drab-grayish yellow with weak, narrow, concentric bands of darker color. Interior ivory. Periostracum gray. Common from Alaska to Puget Sound, and from Greenland to Massachusetts.

Common European Cockle, *Cerastoderma edule* (Linnaeus, 1758). Shell solid, broadly oval, with inrolled beaks almost touching each other. With twenty-two to twenty-eight squarish radial ribs, each with numerous weak scales. Right valve with two

Greenland Cockle
4 in (10 cm)

Nuttall's Cockle
4 in (10 cm)

Iceland Cockle
3 in (7.5 cm)

anterior and two posterior lateral teeth. Interior of valves white and stained brown around the muscle scars. Margins crenulate inside. Abundant near estuaries from Norway to Portugal and West Africa.

Common European Cockle
5 in (12.5 cm)

◆

Trough Clams
(*Family Mactridae*)

Called trough shells in England and surf clams in New England, these large, smooth clams are recognized by the small, spoon-shaped compartment, or chondrophore, in the center of the hinge. Into this fits the pad-like, black resilium which keeps the valves ajar.

California Mactra, *Mactra californica* Conrad, 1837. Shell elongate-oval, moderately fragile, smooth, and with peculiar, concentric undulations on the beaks. The velvety yellowish brown periostracum forms an angular ridge along the top posterior edge of each valve. This small species is fairly common in lagoons of California, but rarer in Puget Sound.

Californian Mactra
2 in (5 cm)

Hooked Surf Clam, *Spisula falcata* (Gould, 1850). Elongate at the narrower anterior end. Low beaks nearer the rounded posterior end. Anterior upper margin

Hooked Surf Clam
2.5 in (6.5 cm)

slightly concave. Exterior chalky, with a brown, shiny periostracum. Common from Washington to California.

Stimpson's Surf Clam, *Spisula polynyma* (Stimpson, 1860). Large, solid. Color dirty-white with a coarse, varnish-like periostracum. Pallial sinus large. Common offshore from the Arctic Seas to Rhode Island; Japan to Puget Sound.

Stimpson's Surf Clam
4 in (10 cm)

Atlantic Surf Clam, *Spisula solidissima* (Dillwyn, 1817). Shell large, strong, elongate-oval and smoothish, except for small, irregular growth lines. Lateral teeth bear very tiny, sawtooth ridges. Color yellowish white with a thin, yellowish brown periostracum. In the hinge, the small oval, black-brown ligament which is close to the dorsal margin does not have a shelly ridge between it and the larger chondrophore cup, as is the case in *Mactra*. An abundant shallow-water, edible species commercially dredged offshore. Occurs from Nova Scotia to off South Carolina.

Atlantic Surf Clam
5 in (12.5 cm)

Alaskan Gaper, *Tresus capax* (Gould, 1850). Shell large, oval-elongate, with a dip or bulge in the ventral margin. Gapes at the posterior end. Cardinal teeth small, and lateral very small. Ligament external and separated from the cartilage pit by a shelly plate. Common in shallow water in sandy mud from Alaska to northern California.

Alaskan Gaper
8 in (20 cm)

Rayed Trough Clam, *Mactra corallina* (Linnaeus, 1758). Shell brittle, ovate; beaks in the midline and curled inward and slightly forward. Color creamy white with purplish around the beaks, and usually with brown rays. Periostracum light-brown. Interior purplish white. Pallial sinus deep. Widely distributed from Norway to the Black Sea and to Senegal.

Rayed Trough Clam
1.5 in (4 cm)

Solid Trough Clam, *Spisula solida* (Linnaeus, 1758). Shell of medium size, solid, ovate, beaks central and the exterior smoothish, except for irregular growth stoppages. Shell whitish gray; periostracum light-brown but usually worn away. Pallial sinus short and rounded at the end. Adductor muscle scars recessed. Hinge teeth strong; with a fairly large chondrophore. Shape of this clam may vary from truncate to oval. Found from 3 to 492 ft (1–150 m) from Finland to Spain and Morocco.

Solid Trough Clam
5 in (12.5 cm)

Subtruncate Trough Clam, *Spisula subtruncata* (da Costa, 1778). Fairly small, ovate-triangular and solid; beaks nearer the front end. Color grayish white to brownish. External ligament is short and narrow just behind the beaks. Sculpture of coarse, concentric lines. Lunule and escutcheon with fine ridges. Laterals finely serrated. Pallial sinus shallow. An abundant offshore sand-lover occurring from Norway to the Black Sea and the Canary Islands.

Subtruncate Trough Clam
1 in (2.5 cm)

Flat Furrow Clam, *Scrobicularia plana* (da Costa, 1778). Shell almost round in outline; compressed; with the beaks almost at the center. Color grayish brown or light-yellow. Periostracum brown, velvety, but usually worn away. Internal ligament large, obliquely slanting and set in the chondrophore. This intertidal clam is in the family Scrobiculariidae. It lives from Norway south to Senegal.

Flat Furrow Clam
2.5 in (6.5 cm)

European Otter Clam, *Lutraria lutraria* (Linnaeus, 1758). Shell fairly large, solid, oval-elongate in outline and gaping at both ends; beaks nearer the front end and directed inward. Color yellowish brown with an olive-brown, thin periostracum. Internal ligament black, triangular and set in a large chondrophore. Pallial sinus large and oval at the closed end. Lower margin of the pallial sinus scar is separated from the pallial line below it. Common from 3 to 295 ft (1–90 m) from Norway to the Baltic, Mediterranean and West Africa.

European Otter Clam
5 in (12.5 cm)

Oblong Otter Clam, *Lutraria magna* (da Costa, 1778). Shell similar to the European Otter Clam, but more elongate, with the dorsal margin behind the beak concave, and with the beaks closer to the front end. The lower section of the pallial sinus is confluent with the main pallial scar. This member of the subfamily Lutrariinae is a common, shallow-water clam living from the British Isles to the Mediterranean.

Oblong Otter Clam
6 in (15 cm)

Arctic Wedge Clam, *Mesodesma arctatum* (Conrad, 1830). Heavy for its size, elongate-oval, with the posterior end truncate and having a very short pallial sinus. Anterior end narrower and compressed. Chondrophore oblique. The lateral teeth have fine, comb-like teeth on each side. Belongs to the family Mesodesmatidae. Common offshore from Greenland and Labrador to Maryland.

Arctic Wedge Clam
1.5 in (4 cm)

Razor Clams
(*Family Pharellidae*)

This widespread family of razorfish or razor clams is predominantly a cold-water group characterized by their elongate and compressed shape, reduced hinge teeth and glossy, smooth periostracum.

Pacific Razor Clam, *Siliqua patula* (Dixon, 1788). Shell light-weight but strong, oval-oblong, laterally compressed. Periostracum varnish-like and olive-green in color. Interior glossy and whitish with a purple flush. Internal rib below the tiny cardinals descend, obliquely towards the anterior ventral margin. An abundant, edible species found in shallow water from Alaska to central California.

Pacific Razor Clam
5 in (12.5 cm)

Squamate Razor Clam, *Siliqua squamata* Blainville, 1827. With a prominent internal rib descending straight down towards the ventral margin. Dull-white with a glossy periostracum with chestnut-brown, concentric bands. Uncommon offshore from Newfoundland to Cape Cod.

Squamate Razor Clam
3 in (7.5 cm)

Atlantic Razor Clam, *Siliqua costata* Say, 1822. Shell delicate, compressed, thin-shelled. Exterior with a shiny, greenish periostracum. Interior glossy, purplish white, with a strong white rib. Very common in shallow water in firm sand from the Gulf of St. Lawrence to off North Carolina.

Atlantic Razor Clam
2 in (5 cm)

Atlantic Jackknife Clam, *Ensis directus* (Conrad, 1843). Shell long, cylindrical, smooth, moderately curved and with sharp edges. Gapes widely at each end. Shell white, covered with a thin, varnish-like, brownish green periostracum. Left valve has two very small, vertical cardinals near the beak end, and each valve has a long, low, inconspicuous posterior lateral tooth. A common, edible species living in sand burrows from southern Labrador to South Carolina, but commonest in New England.

Atlantic Jackknife Clam
9 in (22.5 cm)

Narrow Jackknife Clam, *Ensis ensis* (Linnaeus, 1758). Slightly bowed. Color tan-white with reddish brown blotches. Anterior end rounded. Periostracum greenish brown to yellowish green and glossy. Right valve with one cardinal and two lateral teeth; left valve with two cardinals and two

Narrow Jackknife Clam
4 in (10 cm)

laterals. Fairly common in silty sand from the intertidal zone down to 65 ft (20 m). Ranges from Norway to the Mediterranean.

Giant Razor Clam, *Ensis siliqua* (Linnaeus, 1758). Elongate-rectangular with rounded, gaping ends and almost straight margins. Beaks inconspicuous at the anterior end. Color white with reddish streaks and blotches. Periostracum dark-green. Interior white with purplish tints. This common species is larger and stouter than the Narrow Jackknife Clam. Occurs from Norway to the Baltic and into the Mediterranean.

Giant Razor Clam
8 in (20 cm)

Blunt Jackknife Clam, *Solen sicarius* Gould, 1850. Shell elongate-rectangular, with very slightly curved dorsal and ventral margins. The anterior beak end is obliquely truncate, and the posterior end is rounded and slightly compressed. *Solen* differs from *Ensis* in having only a single tooth usually located at the very anterior end of the valve. Periostracum varnish-like and olive greenish. Common on sandy mud flats from British Columbia to California.

Blunt Jackknife Clam
3.5 in (9 cm)

European Razor Clam, *Solen vagina* Linnaeus, 1758. With parallel margins; obliquely truncate at the anterior end and squarely rounded at the other end. Color yellowish with brownish growth lines. Each valve has one cardinal but no laterals. Synonym is *S. marginatus* Montagu (and Pulteney). This species is found just offshore where it burrows into

European Razor Clam
5 in (12.5 cm)

sandy bottoms. Ranges from Norway into the Baltic and down into the Mediterranean.

Bean Razor Clam, *Pharus legumen* (Linnaeus, 1758). Shell elongate-cylindrical, brittle, with the inconspicuous beaks almost centrally located. Both ends gaping and rounded. Color yellowish white with a yellowish green periostracum. Ligament prominent, external and dark-brown. Right valve with a tiny vertical cardinal and one long, ridge-like anterior lateral and a short, projecting posterior lateral. White rib inside. Pallial sinus short. Common from Norway to the Mediterranean.

Bean Razor Clam
5 in (12.5 cm)

Tellins
(*Family Tellinidae*)

This worldwide family of bivalves is known for its very colorful shells with a simple architecture. Most are smooth, laterally compressed and rather thin-shelled. There is a slight twist at the posterior end. There are two small cardinal teeth, one of which is bifid.

Great Alaskan Tellin, *Tellina lutea* Wood, 1828. Shell strong, elongate-oval, quite compressed laterally and with a posterior twist to the right. Chalky white, commonly with a pink flush.

Great Alaskan Tellin
3.5 in (9 cm)

Periostracum greenish brown.
External ligament prominent.
Pallial sinus three-quarters the
length of the interior. Commonly
found from 3 to 118 ft (1–36 m)
from Japan to Alaska and northern
British Columbia.

Bodegas Tellin, *Tellina bodegensis*
Hinds, 1845. Narrowly elongate,
laterally compressed, with the
posterior end narrow and drawn
out. Dorsal and ventral margins
almost parallel. Pallial line long
and narrow. Exterior with
concentric threads. Fairly common
from 3 to 98 ft (1–30 m) in sand
from Canada to Mexico.

Bodegas Tellin
2 in (5 cm)

Salmon Tellin, *Tellina nuculoides*
(Reeve, 1845). Small, oval, white
with widely spaced growth lines.
Interior with a rose tint. Common
from the Aleutians to central
California.

Story Tellin, *Tellina fabula*
(Gmelin, 1791). Shell small,
elongate-oval, with the posterior
end pointed. Right valve slightly
more convex than the left.
Posterior end twisted towards the
right. Color white or tinged with
yellow or orange. Periostracum
yellowish. Sculpture of concentric
lines. In the left valve diagonal
lines cross them. Pallial sinus deep,
broad, quadrate. Common in sand
3 to 164 ft (1–50 m). Occurs from
Norway to the Black Sea and north
west Africa.

Salmon Tellin
0.5 in (1.2 cm)

Donax Tellin, *Tellina donacina*
Linnaeus, 1758. Shell small, thin-
shelled but strong; right valve
slightly more convex than the left

Story Tellin
0.7 in (2 cm)

one. External ligament large. Color
gray to yellowish with pink rays;
sometimes all-white. Sculpture of
many evenly spaced, concentric
ridges. Interior pearly white with
yellow or pink blush. Pallial sinus
scar almost touches the anterior
adductor muscle. A common,
shallow-water species in coarse
sand from the Orkney
south to the Black Sea and Azores.

Donax Tellin
1 in (2.5 cm)

Thick Tellin, *Arcopagia crassa*
(Pennant, 1777). Circular in
outline; beaks almost in the center;
somewhat compressed. Color dirty
tan with the beaks tinged with
orange or pink radial rays.
Periostracum yellow-brown.
Exterior with concentric ridges
with fine radiating lines showing
between. Common offshore from
Norway to Senegal.

Thick Tellin
2.5 in (6.5 cm)

Chalky Macoma, *Macoma
calcarea* (Gmelin, 1791). Oval-
elongate, moderately compressed,
but somewhat inflated at the larger
anterior end. Beaks three-fifths the
way towards the narrow, slightly
twisted posterior end. *Macoma* do
not have lateral teeth. Gray
periostracum usually worn away
except at margins. Pallial sinus in
left valve does not reach the
anterior muscle scar. Much shorter
in right valve. A common cold-
water species found offshore in
Arctic waters from Greenland to
New York, and from the Bering
Sea to Washington State.

Chalky Macoma
2 in (5 cm)

Balthica Macoma, *Macoma
balthica* (Linnaeus, 1758). Shell
fairly small, oval, moderately
compressed. Color dull whitish,

sometimes flushed with pink. Periostracum thin, gray and flakes off when dry. Pallial sinus reaches halfway to anterior muscle scar in left valve. An abundant intertidal and offshore species in Arctic waters south to estuaries in Norway to Portugal; Greenland to off Georgia.

Balthica Macoma
1 in (2.5 cm

Doleful Macoma, *Macoma moesta* (Deshayes, 1855). Shell ovate, inflated, with the beaks two-thirds the way back from the larger, rounded end. Periostracum yellowish olive. Posterior end short, slightly angular, and finely wrinkled at the angle. Pallial sinus rounded, smaller in right valve. Common offshore in muddy areas. Arctic Seas; Greenland and Alaska.

Doleful Macoma
1.5 in (4 cm)

Tenta Macoma, *Macoma tenta* (Say, 1837). Shell oval-elongate, somewhat compressed, rather fragile. Color white with a delicate iridescence on the smooth exterior. Posterior end slightly twisted to the left. Interior glossy white, tinted with yellow and with fine radiating lines, which produce a finely serrated margin. Two diverging cardinals in the right valve, a single one in the left. A common shallow-water species from Cape Cod to Florida and to Brazil.

Tenta Macoma
0.8 in (2 cm)

Bent-nose Macoma, *Macoma nasuta* (Conrad, 1837). Rather compressed and strongly twisted to the right at the posterior end. Pallial sinus scar in the left valve reaches the anterior muscle scar. External ligament large and black. A very common Pacific coast

Bent-nose Macoma
3 in (7.5 cm)

species living in mud in quiet waters from shore to 164 feet (50 m); southern Alaska to Mexico.

Fouled Macoma, *Macoma inquinata* (Deshayes, 1855). Shell oval-elongate, moderately inflated, very slightly twisted at the posterior end. Pallial sinus in left valve almost reaches the bottom of the anterior muscle scar. Color chalky white. Periostracum gray and with fine concentric growth lines. Posterior ventral margin with a weak embayment. A moderately common, offshore clam ranging from Japan and the Bering Sea to off southern California.

Fouled Macoma
2 in (5 cm)

Sunset Clams
(*Family Psammobiidae*)

These fairly large clams resemble the tellin clams but are generally larger, with purple and reddish colors, and with a large, external ligament that is attached to a prominent, shelly ridge. No lateral teeth. Pallial sinus is large.

Californian Sunset Clam, *Gari californica* (Conrad, 1849). Elongate-oval, fairly strong; the low beaks are nearer the anterior end. Sculpture of strong, irregular, concentric growth lines. Color dirty white or cream, and may have faint, narrow, radial rays of purple. Periostracum brownish

California Sunset Clam
4 in (10 cm)

gray. Common from 3 to 164 ft
(1–50 m), and often washed
ashore after storms. Ranges from
the Aleutians to southern
California.

Depressed Sunset Clam, *Gari
depressa* (Pennant, 1777). Shell
solid, evenly elongate, with the
beaks almost at the center. Right
valve a little more convex. Color
cream with purplish rays.
Periostracum thick and greenish
brown. Lives in coarse sand in 3 to
164 ft (1–50 m). Ranges from the
North Sea to West Africa.

Depressed Sunset Clam
2.5 in (6.5 cm)

Faroes Sunset Clam, *Gari
fervensis* (Gmelin, 1791). Elongate,
with the posterior and narrower
end bearing a rounded keel.
Surface with crowded, concentric
threads. Color of variable purples
and brownish pinks with a few
rays. A common offshore species
from Norway to West Africa.

Faroes Sunset Clam
2 in (5 cm)

Tellin-like Sunset Clam, *Gari
tellinella* (Lamarck, 1818). Shell
small, solid, oval-elongate in
outline. Color whitish cream with
tints of orange, red or purplish.
Periostracum very thin. Ligament
brown with red bands. Sculpture
of fine concentric and radiating
lines. Growth stoppages evident.
Right valve with two bifid
cardinals. No lateral teeth. A
common, shallow-water clam
found from Iceland and Norway to
the Mediterranean.

Tellin-like Sunset Clam
1 in (2.5 cm)

Rose Petal Semele, *Semele
rubropicta* Dall, 1871. In the family
Semelidae, the black resilium is in
an oblique gutter which is buried

in the hinge. Shell oval-elongate, with the beaks nearer the front end. Has irregular growth lines and many radial incised lines. Color chalky gray to tan with faint rays of light-mauve. Interior glossy-white, with mauve at both ends of the hinge. Uncommon offshore. Ranges from Alaska to Mexico.

Rose Petal Semele
1.5 in (4 cm)

White Abra Clam, *Abra alba* (Wood, 1815). Shell small, white, brittle, broadly oval; posterior with a slight twist to the right. Hinge weak and narrow, with the narrow, brown internal ligament in a grooved, triangular chondrophore. Pallial sinus large. Common in mud or muddy gravel from low tide mark to 216 feet (66 m). Ranges from Norway to the Black Sea and to Senegal.

White Abra Clam
0.8 in (2 cm)

Oxheart Clams
(*Family Glossidae*)

Popular as a food and desired by shell collectors, the Oxheart Clam is the only member of this strange family of bivalves in the Northern Hemisphere. The beaks are strongly curled in, and there is no lunule nor any pallial sinus scar.

Oxheart Clam, *Glossus humanus* (Linnaeus, 1758). Shell medium-sized, solid, globular, without any gape, and with strongly enrolled, swollen beaks. Ligament brown and external. Sculpture of fine concentric and radial lines. Exterior tan, sometimes with reddish streaks. Periostracum greenish brown. A common offshore species ranging from Iceland and Norway to the Mediterranean.

Oxheart Clam
3 in (7.5 cm)

Ocean Quahog, *Arctica islandica* (Linnaeus, 1767). Oval in outline, moderately inflated. Color yellowish to brown; periostracum thick, chestnut-brown. No pallial sinus. A common, edible offshore hardshell clam ranging from Iceland to France; Labrador to off North Carolina. In the family Arcticidae.

Ocean Quahog
4 in (10 cm)

Zebra Mussel, *Dreissena polymorpha* (Pallas, 1771). Shell shaped like a *Mytilus* mussel. Anterior muscle attached to a shelf-like platform in the apical region. Byssus strong. Color tan with dark zebra stripes. Common in freshwater in Europe and now in the Great Lakes of United States.

Zebra Mussel
1 in (2.5 cm)

✦

Venus Clams
(*Family Veneridae*)

This is a large and diverse family used extensively for food in many parts of the world. Many have colorful patterns and intricate sculpturing.

Warty Venus, *Venus verrucosa*
Linnaeus, 1758. Circular in
outline and rather swollen. Color
grayish white to brownish cream.
Periostracum brown but usually
worn away. Lunules broad, heart-
shaped, brown, with fine radiating
threads. Escutcheon prominent in
the left valve. Pallial sinus small
and triangular. A common, edible
clam found in shallow water from
the British Isles to the
Mediterranean and Canary
Islands.

Warty Venus
2.5 in (6 cm)

Chamber Venus, *Circomphalus
casinus* (Linnaeus, 1758). Circular
in outline and with numerous,
smooth, raised concentric ridges.
Color whitish tan, sometimes with
reddish brown rays. Inner margin
of valves crenulate. Pallial sinus
short and triangular. A common
offshore species ranging from
Norway to Senegal.

Chamber Venus
2 in (5 cm)

Northern Quahog or Hardshell
Clam, *Mercenaria mercenaria*
(Linnaeus, 1758). Ovate-trigonal,
inflated. Exterior gray with fine
growth threads. Center of valves
are smoothish. Interior white with
purple stains. A common, edible
clam found in shallow water from
Quebec to Texas. Introduced to
California and England.

Northern Quahog
4 in (10 cm)

Common Pacific Littleneck,
Protothaca staminea (Conrad,
1837). Solid, subovate, laterally
compressed, beaks nearer the
anterior end. Sculpture of fine
concentric and radial riblets which
form beads at the anterior end of
the shell. Radial riblets stronger on
the middle of the valves. Lunule

feeble; escutcheon absent. Color rusty-brown with a purplish cast. This common, edible, shallow-water clam is quite variable in sculpturing and coloring. Ranges from the Aleutians to Mexico.

Common Pacific Littleneck
2 in (5 cm)

Filipino Venus or Japanese Littleneck, *Ruditapes philippinarum* (Adams and Reeve, 1850). Subovate, laterally compressed, with beaks nearer the anterior end. Lunule smooth and incised. Escutcheon smooth and bordered by a low ridge. With radial threads, those at posterior end beaded. Interior purplish. This eastern Asian species was introduced to Puget Sound and California.

Filipino Venus
2 in (5 cm)

Decussate Venus or Carpet-shell, *Venerupis decussata* (Linnaeus, 1758). Broadly oval, with numerous radial riblets crossed by fine concentric growth lines. Colors of grays, yellows and browns, sometimes with rays and streaks. Interior glossy white with an orange tinge, rarely purplish. Pallial sinus deep. Margin smooth. Common in shallow water from Norway to Mediterranean.

Decussate Venus
2 in (5 cm)

Morrhua Venus, *Pitar morrhuanus* Linsley, 1848. Shell small, obese, oval-elongate, with a large, elongate lunule. Beaks large and towards the anterior end. Anterior left lateral fits into a well-developed socket in the right valve. Middle left cardinal large; posterior right cardinal bifid. Exterior dull-gray to brownish red, with numerous heavy lines of growth. This is a fairly common offshore clam ranging from the

Morrhua Venus
1 in (2.5 cm)

Gulf of St. Lawrence to off North
Carolina where it serves as an
important food for bottom fish.

Smooth Washington Clam,
Saxidomus gigantea (Deshayes,
1839). Solid, oblong, heavy, with
fairly coarse, crowded concentric
threads and fine growth stoppages.
Valves gape slightly at the back
end. Hinge with four or five
cardinal teeth in the right valve,
four in the left. Pallial sinus long
and fairly narrow. No lunule.
Ligament large. Color grayish
white. A common food clam in
Alaska. Extends southward to
northern California.

**Smooth Washington
Clam**
3 in (7.5 cm)

Wolf Dosinia, *Dosinia lupinus*
(Poli, 1791). Shell solid, circular in
outline, moderately compressed.
Beaks in front of the midline.
Ligament deeply inset. Lunule
short, heart-shaped and with fine
radial ridges. Sculpture of fine
concentric ridges crossed by faint
radiating lines. Three cardinal
teeth in each valve. Pallial sinus
triangular, deep. Margin smooth.
Lives in sand and silty mud from 3
to 426 ft (1–130 m) from Iceland
and Norway to the Mediterranean
and south to West Africa.

Wolf Dosinia
1.5 in (4 cm)

Mature Dosinia, *Dosinia exoleta*
(Linnaeus, 1758). Shell circular
and laterally compressed. Similar
to the Wolf Dosinia, but the lunule
is flatter, the valves are flatter, the
pallial sinus is larger and broader
and the exterior is not as glossy.
The color is light-brown, with
numerous fine, radial, reddish
brown streaks, usually
accumulating at former growth

Mature Dosinia
2 in (5 cm)

stoppages. While buried in sand, it leaves two small round holes marking the presence of the two siphons. The clam occurs from the intertidal zone down to about 229 ft (70 m) of water. It has a wide range, from Norway to Portugal, into the Mediterranean, and south to Senegal and Gabon.

Kennerley's Venus, *Humilaria kennerleyi* (Reeve, 1863). Shell fairly large, elongate-oval, laterally compressed. Beaks near the smaller, anterior end. Exterior with sharp, neatly spaced, concentric ribs whose edges are bent upwards. Color and texture resembles gray Portland cement. Margin of shell finely crenulate. A fairly common collector's item occurring offshore from 19 to 98 ft (6–30 m) from Alaska to northern California.

Kennerley's Venus
3.5 in (9 cm)

Hearty Ruppellaria, *Rupellaria carditoides* (Conrad, 1837). Oblong-ovate, obese, solid, pure-white. Variable in shape because it bores into hard rock. Exterior chalky grayish white with coarse, irregular, concentric growth lines. Radial sculpture of peculiar, fine, scratched lines crowded together. No lunule or escutcheon. Hinge without lateral teeth. Three cardinals in the left valve; two in right valve. Pallial sinus well-developed. Nepionic shell at beak is oblong. Common in rocks in shallow water from Vancouver Island to Baja California, Mexico.

Hearty Rupellaria
1.5 in (4 cm)

False Angel Wing, or American Piddock, *Petricola pholadiformis* (Lamarck, 1818). Shell elongate, rather fragile and chalky-white.

Numerous radial ribs; the anterior ten or so are larger and bear prominent scales. Ligament external and located just posterior to the beaks. Cardinal teeth quite long and pointed. A very common clay and peat-moss borer. Rarely in limestone in Europe. Frequents estuaries. Ranges from the Gulf of St. Lawrence to Texas and south to Uruguay; introduced to western Europe where it has spread from Norway to West Africa.

False Angel Wing
2 in (5 cm)

Arctic Saxicave, *Hiatella arctica* (Linnaeus, 1767). Shell chalky-white, oblong, usually somewhat misshapen because it bores into rocks and small boulders. No definite teeth in the thickened hinge of adults. Pallial line discontinuous. Periostracum gray and thin. Sometimes with a radial rib at the posterior end, which may bear scales. Common also in kelp holdfasts and rock crevices subtidally. Arctic Seas to California; Labrador to Uruguay; Norway to the Mediterranean and Azores.

Arctic Saxicave
2 in (5 cm)

◆

Sand-gapers or Soft-shell Clams
(*Family Myidae*)

The gapers, or soft-shell clams, are popular seafood in the Northern Hemisphere, both in the New World and Old World.

The chalky, white shells are easily broken. The valves gape at the posterior end where a long, fused pair of siphons extend.

Sand-gaper, or Soft-shell Clam, *Mya arenaria* Linnaeus, 1758. Shell chalky, brittle, elliptical, oblong, and gaping at the posterior end. Color white to grayish, with a thin gray to straw periostracum. Chondrophore in left valve is long, spoon-shaped and shallow. An abundant, intertidal, mud or sand flat species fished commercially in New England. It has a wide range from southern Labrador to off North Carolina; from northern Norway to France and from Alaska to northern California.

Sand-gaper
4 in (10 cm)

Blunt Gaper, or Truncate Soft-shell Clam, *Mya truncata* Linnaeus, 1758. Shell similar to the Sand-gaper, but smaller, abruptly truncate at the posterior siphonal end, and the lower margin of the pallial line is confluent with the pallial sinus scar. A common Arctic species found offshore south to Massachusetts, Portugal, Washington State and Japan.

Blunt Gaper
2.5 in (6.5 cm)

Common Basket-shell, or Fat Corbula, *Corbula gibba* (Olivi, 1792). Shell small, solid, with the right valve deeper and larger than the left one which fits into it. Left valve with chondrophore and a deep triangular pit. Pallial sinus absent. Color cream, with a brownish periostracum. In family Corbulidae.

Common Basket-shell
0.5 in (1.2 cm)

Geoduck (goo-ee-duck), *Panopea abrupta* (Conrad, 1849). Shell large, inflated, elongate, thick-shelled and gaping at both ends. Coarse, concentric, wavy lines especially noticeable near the small, central, depressed beaks. Periostracum thin and yellowish. Exterior dirty-white to cream; interior semi-glossy white. Hinge with a single, large, horizontal thickening. Common in mud 2 or 3 ft (60–90 cm). Ranges from Alaska to the Gulf of California, but commercially fished in Washington and Oregon.

Geoduck
9 in (22.5 cm)

European Piddock, *Pholas dactylus* Linnaeus, 1758. Shell brittle, elongate, gaping at both ends; umbones near the anterior end and covered with two elongate, separate, calcareous protoplax plates. On the back edge is the small, central mesoplax, and posterior to that is the long, narrow, calcareous, metaplax plate. Within the valve and under the umbonal reflection is the long, narrow, projecting apophysis. Anterior end of valve with about forty spined, radiating ribs. Remainder of valve with concentric ridges. Pallial sinus scar wide and shallow. Bores into many subtidal substrates, including sand, peat, wood, shale and sandstone. Ranges from Norway to the Black Sea and from Labrador to Delaware.

European Piddock
5 in (12.5 cm)

Paper Piddock, *Pholadidea loscombiana* Turton, 1819. Shell fragile, elongate-oval, divided into two regions by the umbonal-ventral sulcus. Gaping anterior end may be sealed over by a smooth, bulbous callum. Tooth-like apophyses are small, fragile and project from beneath the umbones. Edge of wide gape is serrated. Pallial sinus broad and deep. Common in clay, peat and sandstone in British Isles and coast of France.

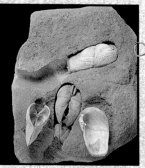

Paper Piddock
1 in (2.5 cm)

Striate Nartesia, *Martesia striata* (Linnaeus, 1758). Variable in shape, usually pear-shaped, producing a round, smooth callum over the wide foot-gape in the adult. Posterior end compressed and rounded in outline. Anterior to the oblique external furrow are numerous, finely denticulate riblets. White in color, with a tan periostracum. Sculpture of fine concentric parallel threads. Apophyses long, thin. Pallial sinus deep. Common in floating or submerged wood from North Carolina south to Brazil. Introduced to the British Isles.

Striate Martesia
1 in (2.5 cm)

Gabb's Piddock, *Penitella gabbi* (Tryon, 1863). Shell thin but strong, elongate-oval, with an oblique, external sulcus, in front of which is the wide, oblique gape for the foot. Anterior end with numerous radial, beaded ribs. Mesoplax plate in the adult has broad, lateral wings. Siphonoplax absent. Moderately common in clay and sandstone. Ranges from Drier Bay, Alaska, to San Pedro, California.

Gabb's Piddock
2 in (5 cm)

Gould's Shipworm, *Bankia gouldi* Bartsch, 1908. There are many species of *Teredo* and *Bankia* shipworms throughout the Northern Hemisphere, and a scientific monograph must be consulted in order properly to identify them. The drilling is done by a pair of cup-like shelly valves. The soft parts of the bivalve are encased in long, shelly, white tunnels. The exit to the water is protected by a pair of "feathery" pallets. The latter are used in identifying species. Great destruction to wooden ships and wharf pilings done by shipworms and by the crustacean, *Limnoria*.

**Gould's Shipworm
Tubes**
8 in (20 cm)

✦

Acknowledgments

The author wishes to thank the curators and staff of the Departments of Mollusks at the Museum of Comparative Zoology, Harvard University; the Academy of Natural Sciences of Philadelphia and the U.S. National Museum in Washington D.C., for their kindness in permitting him to study and photograph the molluscs under their care.

The publisher wishes to thank the following photographers for their illustrations which appear on pages 15 and 119: David Parmiter; pages 6 and 36/7: Nigel Downer, Planet Earth Pictures; page 110/11: John Downer, Planet Earth Pictures; page 115: Robert A. Jureit, Planet Earth Pictures.

Bibliography

A small field guide to the molluscs of three major faunal areas in the northern hemisphere will cover just a few of the thousands of known species. This bibliography will lead you to major reference books and specialized monographs that deal with certain families. Annual listings of the world's literature on molluscs is cross-referenced by subject matter in *The Zoological Record*, section 9 on *Mollusca*, London and Philadelphia.

Northeastern Pacific

Abbott, R. Tucker 1974, *American Seashells*. 2nd ed., 663 pp., (about 3000 figs), Van Nostrand Reinhold, New York.

Bernard, F. R. 1979, Bivalve Mollusks of the Western Beaufort Sea [Alaska]. In *Sci. Nat. Hist. Mus. Los Angeles Co.*, no. 313, pp. 1-80, (109 figs).

Bernard, F. R. 1983, *Catalogue of the Living Bivalvia of the Eastern Pacific Ocean: Bering Strait to Cape Horn*. Canadian Special Publ. Fish. Aquat. Sci., vol. 61, 102 pp.

MacGinitie, N. 1959, Marine Mollusca of Point Barrow, Alaska. *Proc. U.S. Nat. Mus.*, vol. 109, pp. 59-208.

McLean, James H. 1969, *Marine Shells of Southern California*. 104 pp., (illus.), Los Angeles County Mus. Nat. Hist., Zoology no. 11, Los Angeles.

Rice, Thomas C. 1968, *A Checklist of the Marine Gastropods from the Puget Sound Region*. 169 pp. Of Sea and Shore Publ., Port Gamble, Washington.

Western Atlantic

Abbott, R. Tucker, 1974, *American Seashells*. 2nd ed., 663 pp., (24 pls, 3000 text figs), Van Nostrand Reinhold Co., New York.

Abbott, R. Tucker, 1986, *Seashells of North America*. Revised ed., 280 pp., (illus.), Golden Press, New York.

Bousefield, E. L. 1960, *Canadian Atlantic Shells*. 72 pp. National Mus. Ottawa, Canada.

Clench, William J., (ed.) 1941-74, *Johnsonia* - Monographs of the Marine Mollusks of the Western Atlantic, vols. 1-5, nos. 1-50. Harvard Univ., Cambridge, Massachusetts.

Eastern Atlantic

Ankel, W. E. 1936, Prosobranchia. In *Die Tierwelt der Nord- und Ostsee*. Vol, IX bl. Akadem. Verlagsgesell., Leipzig.

Bouchet, P, Danrigal, F. and Huyghens, C. 1978, *Coquillage des Côtes atlantiques et de la Manche*. Editions du Pacifique, Paris.

Fretter, V. and Graham. A. 1962, *British Prosobranch Molluscs*. 755 pp. Ray Society, London.

Graham, Alastair 1988, *Molluscs: Prosobranch and Pyramidellid Gastropods*. 2nd ed. 662 pp., (276 text figs). E. J. Brill/Dr. W. Backhuys, Leiden.

McMillan, Nora F. 1968, *British Shells*. 196 pp., (80 pls.-32 in colour, 144 illus.pgs). Frederick Warne & Co., London and New York.

Nordsieck, Fritz 1968-69, *Die europaischen Meeresmuscheln* (vol. 1, Prosobranchia; vol. 2, Bivalvia; vol. 3, Opisthobranchia). G. Fischer, Stuttgart.

Parenzan, Pietro 1970-76, *Carta d'identita delle conchiglie del Mediterraneo*. Vol. 1 Gastropdoi; vol. 2, pts 1 and 2, Bivalvi. Ed. Bios Taras, Taranto.

Tebble, Norman 1976, *British Bivalve Seashells*. 2nd ed. 212 pp., (12 pls, 110 text figs). Royal Scottish Mus., Edinburgh.

Thompson, T. E. and Brown, G. H. 1976, *British Opisthobranch Molluscs*. 203 pp. Synopses of the British Fauna (New Series), no. 8. Academic Press, London and New York.

van Benthem Jutting, W. S. S. 1959, The Netherlands as an environment for molluscan life. *Basteria*, vol. 23, supplement, 174 pp. Leiden.

General and Special Groups

Breisch, L. L. and Kennedy, V. S. 1980, *A Selected Bibliography of Worldwide Oyster Literature*. 309 pp. Univ. Maryland, Maryland.

Kaas, P. and Van Belle, R. A. 1980, *Catalogue of Living Chitons*. 144 pp. E. J. Brill/Dr. W. Backhuys, Leiden.

Kaas, P. and Van Belle, R. A. 1985-87, *Monograph of Living Chitons*. Vols. 1-3. E. J. Brill/ Dr. W. Backhuys, Leiden.

Lalli, Carol M. and Gilmer, Ronald W. 1989, *Pelagic Snails: The Biology of Holoplanktonic Gastropod Mollusks*. 259 pp., (76 text figs). Stanford University Press, California.

Moore, R. C. (ed.). 1960-69, *Treatise on Invertebrate Paleontology*. Part I (Gastropoda), Part N, vols. 1 and 2 (Bivalvia). Geol. Soc. America, Boulder, Colorado.

Morton, J. E. 1976, *Molluscs*. 4th ed. 244 pp., (41 text figs). Hutchinson & Co., London.

Thompson, T. E. 1976, *Biology of Opisthobranch Molluscs*. Vol. 1, 207 pp. Ray Society, London.

Thompson, T. E. and Brown, G. H. 1984, *Biology of Opisthobranch Molluscs*. Vol. 2, 229 pp. (41 coloured pls), Ray Society, London.

Turner, Ruth D. 1966, *A Survey and Illustrated Catalogue of the Teredinidae*. 265 pp., (64 pls), Mus. Comp. Zool., Harvard Univ., Cambridge, Massachusetts.

Yonge, C. M. and Thompson, T. E. 1976, *Living Marine Molluscs*. 288 pp., (16 pls, 162 text figs). Collins, London.

Index